OXFORD
INDIA SHORT
INTRODUCTIONS
**EMPLOYMENT IN
INDIA**

The Oxford India Short
Introductions are concise,
stimulating, and accessible guides
to different aspects of India.
Combining authoritative analysis,
new ideas, and diverse perspectives,
they discuss subjects which are
topical yet enduring, as also
emerging areas of study and debate.

T0364634

SOME OTHER TITLES IN THE SERIES

Indian Federalism
Loiuse Tillin

Surrogacy
Anindita Majumdar

Jawaharlal Nehru
Rudrangshu Mukherjee

The Partition of India
Haimanti Roy

Indian Nuclear Policy
Harsh V. Pant and Yogesh Joshi

Indian Democracy
Suhas Palshikar

Indian National Security
Chris Ogden

Bollywood
M.K. Raghavendra

The Indian Middle Class
Surinder S. Jodhka and Aseem Prakash

Indian Foreign Policy
Sumit Ganguly

Dalit Assertion
Sudha Pai

For more information, visit our website:
https://india.oup.com/content/series/o/
oxford-india-short-introductions/

OXFORD
INDIA SHORT
INTRODUCTIONS

EMPLOYMENT IN INDIA

AJIT KUMAR GHOSE

OXFORD
UNIVERSITY PRESS

OXFORD
UNIVERSITY PRESS

Oxford University Press is a department of the University of Oxford.
It furthers the University's objective of excellence in research, scholarship,
and education by publishing worldwide. Oxford is a registered trademark of
Oxford University Press in the UK and in certain other countries.

Published in India by
Oxford University Press
22 Workspace, 2nd Floor, 1/22 Asaf Ali Road, New Delhi 110 002

ISBN-13 (print edition): 978-0-19-012097-9
ISBN-10 (print edition): 0-19-012097-5

ISBN-13 (eBook): 978-0-19-099006-0
ISBN-10 (eBook): 0-19-099006-6

Typeset in 11/14.3 Bembo Std
by The Graphics Solution, New Delhi 110 092
Printed in India at Replika Press Pvt. Ltd

For
Ruchira and Paroma

Contents

Tables, Figures, and Boxes

Tables

Figures

Boxes

Abbreviations

DGET	Directorate General of Employment and Training
EQI	employment quality index
GDP	gross domestic product
IT	information technology
MGNREGS	Mahatma Gandhi National Rural Employment Guarantee Scheme
NDP	net domestic product
NSSO	National Sample Survey Office
UN	United Nations

Acknowledgement

The author gratefully acknowledges the invaluable assistance of Abhishek Kumar in organizing the statistical data for the book.

1

Introduction

Employment is engagement in productive and income-yielding work, that is, work that contributes to production of goods and services on the one hand and generates income for the person engaged in that work on the other. Employment, therefore, constitutes the critical link between wealth and welfare, between economic growth and improvement in the level of living of the population in a country. Economic growth lifts living standards of the mass of population when it is associated with substantial expansion of employment opportunities for the adult population.

But economic growth does not always bring about improvement in employment conditions. That is why economic growth is not the same thing as economic development, which means sustained improvement in material conditions of life of the population in a country. Improvement in material conditions of life requires expanding production of goods and services on the one hand and simultaneously increasing access of the population to those goods and services on the other. The latter can only be realized if there is increasing remunerative engagement of the mass of adult population in bringing about that expansion of production. In other words, improvement in material conditions occurs when people are engaged as both producers and consumers in a process of economic expansion. Economic development is economic growth with employment.

Because it does not necessarily bring about improvement in employment conditions, economic growth without economic development is perfectly possible. In economic history, there are many instances of economic growth not affecting the living standards of a large majority of the population or even of actually worsening them. In India too, as we shall see, there have been episodes of economic growth without development. This is why development strategies cannot just be growth strategies; they must be 'growth with employment' strategies.

At the time of Independence, India inherited a low-income dual economy, which was composed of a small modern (also called organized or formal) sector and a large traditional (also called unorganized or informal) sector. Employment conditions were very poor. This was reflected not in high unemployment—most people could not afford to be unemployed—but in the very small share of the modern sector (where jobs were of reasonable quality) in total employment, in substantial underemployment of many of the employed, in widespread engagement in low-productivity activities, and in mass poverty. Given this context, as India embarked on planned development, employment naturally became a major area of focus for its development planners.

All the successive growth strategies and policy regimes implemented in India have avowedly sought to address the employment problem. Yet, employment remains a major area of concern even today, after 70 years of India's pursuit of economic development. Very significant economic growth has been achieved; real per capita income in 2017/18 was more than seven times what it had been in 1950/51. But the improvement in material conditions of the mass of population has been far more modest. The reason is that economic growth has not brought about commensurate improvement in employment conditions. The share of the modern sector in total employment in the country is still small; underemployment of the employed is still substantial; engagement in low-productivity activities is still widespread; and mass poverty still exists.

What all this underlines is the weak link between economic growth and employment that has characterized India's experience. Why has the link been weak? The argument presented in this book points to the failure to promote manufacturing-led growth as the main reason. Manufacturing did lead the growth process in the first phase of India's growth, which spanned the period from the mid-1950s till the end-1970s. But capital- and skill-intensive heavy industries dominated manufacturing and the possibility of export-led growth of manufacturing was simply ruled out. In consequence, the potential developmental benefits of manufacturing, which arise from the existence of increasing returns to scale in production and the ability to employ low-skilled labour at a productivity premium, remained unrealized. In the absence of exports, production could not be on a scale large enough for the realization of increasing returns to scale. Moreover, the emphasis on capital- and skill-intensive manufacturing ruled out expanding the employment of low-skilled labour.

At the end of the first phase, services replaced manufacturing as the lead sector in the growth process. But, unlike in most countries of the world, the employment intensity of services in India has not just been low but has also been declining. While in most countries the share of services in gross domestic product

(GDP) roughly equals their share in employment, the former is double the latter in India. And the growth of services has been led by skill-intensive services so that the overall employment intensity has been declining. India's services-led growth, consequently, has been a poor generator of employment. Economic growth, it turns out, has throughout been biased against the use of labour, particularly against the use of low-skilled labour, the supply of which has been and remains abundant.

India's services-led growth has attracted wide attention because it is so exceptional. Economic history shows that growth had been manufacturing-led at early stages of development in all countries that have succeeded in achieving economic transformation. India alone seems to have defied this historical pattern in achieving rapid services-led growth at a rather early stage of its development. This has led some economists to view this as a twenty-first century phenomenon when the digital revolution has transformed certain services and has made them somewhat similar to manufacturing.

The facts examined in this book point to a very different view of the phenomenon. They suggest that India's services-led growth has rested on rather fragile foundations and is unlikely to be sustained for much longer. For, contrary to a widespread impression,

India's services-led growth has not been sustained by rapid export-oriented growth of those services, which have been transformed by the digital revolution. The only services of the kind that have witnessed export-oriented growth are software services. Even in 2005, after years of rapid growth, these services accounted for 4 per cent of India's total services output and just 2 per cent of its GDP. The figures would obviously have been far smaller in the early 1980s when the period of services-led growth began. With such small weights, these services could hardly have been a powerful engine of growth.

At any rate, we know that the rapid growth of services has in fact been led by domestic demand and has involved rapid growth of non-traded services. This is the main puzzle. At low levels of per capita income—and India's per capita income is low even today—it is the demand for manufactures and not the demand for services that is expected to grow rapidly. Yet, in India, it is the demand for services that has grown rapidly. How is this to be explained? The only possible explanation lies in high and growing inequality of income distribution. We now know that income inequality started to increase from the early 1980s and increased particularly sharply post 1992.

On close scrutiny it becomes clear that India's services-led growth has actually been the visible face of what in essence has been foreign-finance-led growth. On the demand side, inflows of foreign finance have been generating incomes for the already rich thereby rapidly increasing income inequality; and this pattern of income growth has been generating rapid growth of domestic demand for services. On the supply side, these inflows have been financing the growing trade deficit, itself the result of the services-led growth, leading to a growing shortfall in production of goods required for consumption and investment. This kind of services-led growth is unlikely to be sustained for long for two reasons. First, its sustenance requires financing of a growing trade deficit and hence depends crucially on sustenance of foreign finance inflow at appropriate levels. This cannot be taken as guaranteed since it will be determined by developments in the global economy. Second, continued growth of income inequality cannot but lead to decelerating growth of aggregate demand in the economy, thereby bringing about slowdown of growth.

It is also crucially important to recognize that even if this kind of services-led growth is somehow sustained, it will not help meet the formidable employment challenge that India is confronted with. To achieve even a modest goal of reaching a situation of zero surplus labour (that is, no underemployment and unemployment) by 2035, around 11 million productive

7

non-agricultural jobs will need to be created annually. Moreover, a large proportion of these jobs will have to be for low-skilled workers. Millions of such workers are already in the labour force but are either seriously underemployed or engaged in very low-productivity activities and millions more will be joining the labour force every year. Past experience shows that services-led growth, even when it is rapid, simply cannot generate non-agricultural jobs of this kind and magnitude.

A transition from services-led growth to manufacturing-led growth will be required to meet the employment challenge. It is rapid growth of manufacturing that can bring rapid growth of jobs, particularly for low-skilled workers. Rapid growth of manufacturing can also contribute indirectly by increasing the employment intensity of services growth and by stimulating growth of construction, a low-skilled employment-intensive industry.

Moreover, manufacturing-led growth can be expected to be faster than services-led growth, and this too will obviously help in meeting the employment challenge. One reason is to be found in the traditional strengths of manufacturing—increasing returns to scale in production and strong spillover effects on other sectors of the economy. A second reason is that given India's low level of industrialization, the scope for growth of manufacturing is large. That growth of manufacturing will reduce the trade deficit so that foreign capital can finance investment rather than trade deficit is a third reason.

These are the kinds of issues, concerns, and arguments that this book seeks to explore and develop. The book is written in non-technical language, avoiding use of economists' jargons as far as possible, so as make it accessible to the non-specialist reader. But it is based on serious research and the specialist reader will also find in it facts and arguments to engage with. Employment is an area of widespread concern. Most people instinctively know that India has a serious employment problem, but very few know its nature. Most people also feel that employment conditions in the country are not that much better today than what they were at the point of India's emergence as an independent nation, but very few know how and why. Most people want the employment conditions to improve speedily in future, but very few have any idea as to how this might happen. This book, hopefully, will bring better understanding and food for thought to all of them.

Four chapters follow this introductory chapter. Chapter 2 discusses some concepts and definitions that are used in discourses on employment and unemployment. It also outlines an appropriate conceptual framework for examining the state of employment and the process of change in an economy such as India's. This conceptual framework is used in Chapter 3 to develop an empirical view of the employment conditions and their evolution over a period of more than six decades. A basic message that this exercise delivers is that the improvement in employment conditions over this long period has been surprisingly small. Since India's growth performance has been quite impressive at least since the early 1980s, a disconnect between growth and employment is evident. Chapter 4 then investigates why and how such a disconnect arose. It first provides a broad review of the phases and characteristics of economic growth over the period since the mid-1950s and then delves into the reasons why growth failed to bring commensurate improvement in employment conditions. Chapter 5, the concluding chapter, first develops a perspective on the jobs challenge that India is confronted with and must respond to. It then goes on to discuss the change of growth strategy that will be required to meet the challenge in the not-too-distant future.

2

Nature and Characteristics

Employment and unemployment are such widely used terms that it might seem superfluous to define them. Yet, wide usage does not mean that the concepts are well understood. Economists need to have a clear definition of terms in order to conduct analysis at both conceptual and empirical levels, and statisticians need this for purposes of measurement.

However, even when there are generally accepted definitions, the meaning of employment and unemployment remain somewhat context-specific. In particular, they do not mean the same things in less developed economies as in advanced economies.

This chapter begins with a brief discussion of the definitions of employment and related concepts. It then considers the meanings of the concepts in the specific context of India's economy and, following on this, outlines an appropriate framework of analysis of issues, problems, and trends. It concludes with a discussion of interrelationships among employment, economic growth, and development.

What Is Employment?

Employment is engagement in economically gainful activities, which are defined by what is known as the 'third person rule'. According to this rule, an activity is economically gainful if it is of such character that it might be delegated to a paid worker. The rule effectively delineates activities that generate measurable output on the one hand and incomes for the persons engaged on the other. There are a few activities, however, that defy neat classification. Activities such as cooking, cleaning or caring for children, sick and elderly are economically gainful by the 'third person rule'; indeed, they are often performed by paid workers. But, by convention, engagement in such activities by family members is not regarded as employment, essentially because of the ambiguities involved in valuation of the output as also of the labour employed.[1] Since such activities are performed primarily by female members of households, much of women's work fails to get counted as employment, a fact that has generated heated debates and controversies. There are other activities such as begging and prostitution, which do not satisfy the 'third person rule' even though they clearly generate measurable incomes for the persons engaged; engagement in these activities is also not regarded as employment.

Unemployment, of course, is lack of employment. But not all persons who are without employment can be regarded as unemployed because not all of them need be interested in being employed. Only those persons who currently are not in employment but are seeking or available for employment are regarded as unemployed. The employed (also called the workforce) and the unemployed together constitute the labour force. Persons who are not in employment but are also not seeking or are not available for employment are considered to be out of the labour force.

Employment can be of two basic types: wage employment, engagement in work for pay in the form of wage or salary, and self-employment, engagement in work in own enterprise, which generates output and income that accrue to the person engaged. Wage employment itself can be of two sub-types: regular wage employment—long-term employment with a fixed employer, specified space and time for work, and a fixed salary paid periodically (in general, monthly); and casual wage employment—employment on a daily basis for a daily wage with no fixed employer or place of work. Regular wage employment can also be of two kinds: formal employment—regular wage-paid jobs that come with entitlement to some kind of social security benefit; and simply regular employment—regular wage-paid jobs with no entitlement to any kind of social security benefit. Persons in self-employment fall into three categories: employers, who run their own enterprises and work in them but also regularly hire wage-paid workers; own-account workers, who run and work in their own enterprises but do not usually hire wage-paid workers; and unpaid family workers, members of families of employers and own-account workers who work in their enterprises but do not receive any payment, though, as family members, they share in the incomes from the enterprises.

Employment and Unemployment in India

At the time of Independence, India was what economists refer to as a labour-surplus dual economy.[2] As we shall see, India's economy remains a labour-surplus dual economy to this day. Employment and unemployment have certain special characteristics in such an economy and a proper understanding of these characteristics is of much importance in studying the current state of and past trends in conditions of employment.

In schematic terms, a labour-surplus dual economy is composed of two distinct sectors: a small modern (also called formal or organized) sector and a large traditional (also called informal or unorganized) one. We choose to use the terms 'modern' and 'traditional' throughout this book. In the modern sector, capital—a set of produced means of production, for example, buildings, machinery, and equipment used to produce goods and services—is an important factor of production, the producers are capitalistic entrepreneurs (including state agencies) who hire workers and employ them together with capital (machines, buildings, and raw materials) for production, and the motivation for production is profit. In the traditional sector, little capital is used in production, natural resources are of much importance, the producers are self-employed (who may or may not be using hired casual labour), and the motivation for production is consumption.

The characteristics of employment in the two sectors are quite different. The principal type of employment in the modern sector is regular wage employment, formal or simply regular. In the traditional sector, self-employment and casual wage employment are the dominant types. Labour productivity (output per worker) is naturally much higher in the modern sector, where capital is in use, than in the traditional sector, where little or no capital is in use. The large difference in productivity translates into a significant difference in earning from employment; wage per unit of work in the modern sector is much higher than earning per unit of work of self-employed persons and casual workers in the traditional sector. One consequence of this 'wage gap' is that for the modern sector, labour supply is virtually unlimited, that is, much in excess of demand at any point of time. For, together with the fresh entrants into the labour force, many of the workers currently employed in the traditional sector would readily move to jobs in the modern sector whenever such jobs become available since they can derive large benefits from such a move.

Surplus labour—presently unutilized but potentially utilizable labour—naturally cannot exist to any significant extent in the modern sector, where capitalistic entrepreneurs hire workers only as they need and employment is generally full-time. It is the traditional sector that serves as the reservoir of surplus labour, which exists in the form of underemployment of the employed and not in the form of visible or open unemployment.

As there is no institutionalized social assistance available to them, workers in the traditional sector must work to survive even if the work they can find is neither very productive nor very remunerative. They simply cannot afford to be unemployed. On the other hand, the dominant systems of employment in the traditional sector—self-employment and casual wage employment—offer much scope for work-sharing, whereby a given volume of work can be performed by a flexible number of workers. In self-employment, the working members of a household share the work in and the income from the household enterprise; additional workers in households can simply become additional sharers of both work and income. In casual wage employment, workers seek employment on a daily basis and get hired by different employers on different days. It is also the case that there is perennial excess supply in casual labour markets. This condition is in fact necessary for the casual labour system to function. For employers cannot rely on this type of labour unless they can be sure of its availability whenever they need to hire labour. The condition of perennial excess supply of course means that not all casual workers get hired on any particular day. But while some fail to get hired on any given day, no one fails to get hired on all days. A given amount of wage-paid work is thus shared by a larger than required number of casual workers. An increase in their number, then, can simply mean additional sharers of the given amount of wage-paid work available.

The existence of surplus labour, therefore, means underemployment of casual workers and self-employed persons, many of whom involuntarily end up working only part-time; the total volume of work they perform could have been performed by fewer persons working full-time. Hence, if some of the self-employed and casual workers move out of the traditional sector and find jobs in the modern sector, those remaining in the traditional sector can work additional days or hours so that the level of underemployment declines but not the amount of labour actually employed in production. So, a decline in the number of workers in the traditional sector means fuller employment and higher output per worker but not a decline in total output. By the same token, an increase in the number of workers in the traditional sector means higher underemployment and lower output per worker but not a rise in total output.

To the extent that it exists, unemployment in a labour-surplus dual economy reflects queuing by the educated youth for jobs in the modern sector. In the absence of institutionalized social assistance programmes, only the youth from relatively well-off households can afford to acquire education above a certain level and can also afford to wait in the queue for jobs since their families have the means to support them through a waiting period, which of course is uncertain length. Unemployment, therefore, is small and the unemployed are economically better-off than many of the employed. Indeed, many of the employed in the traditional sector are poor. The combination of low labour productivity and underemployment produces mass poverty of the employed in the traditional sector.

Empirical evidence on these features of employment and unemployment in India's economy will be more fully explored in Chapter 3. Here, we can cite some facts to illustrate the conditions existing at the start of India's journey of development.[3] In 1955, the first year for which some relevant statistical data are available, less than 7 per cent of the employed was in formal employment in the modern sector. On the other hand, 72 per cent of the employed was in self-employment and the remaining 21 per cent was in non–formal wage employment, mostly in casual wage employment. The unemployment rate (the number unemployed as per cent of the number in the labour force) was just over 1 per cent and the unemployed were mostly persons with some education. Thus, persons with at least secondary education constituted just 1 per cent of the labour force but 21 per cent of the unemployed. Also, the unemployment rate was just 1 per cent for persons with below secondary education but 22 per cent for persons with at least secondary education. Underemployment of the employed, on the other hand, was high; 33 per cent of the employed persons, for example, worked for less than 15 days in a 30-day period. Poverty was widespread; more than 50 per cent of the population lived in poverty and the poor belonged almost exclusively to households of those employed in the traditional sector.[4]

Dualism and the Production Sectors

Thus far, our focus has been on the characterization of India's economy as a labour-surplus dual economy. But India's economy, like any other economy, is composed of distinct production sectors such as agriculture, manufacturing, services, and so on. It is necessary, therefore, to understand the nature of the relationship that exists between dualism and surplus labour on the one hand and the structure of the economy in terms of production sectors on the other. This relationship can be discerned from the structure of employment in different production sectors once it is recognized (*a*) that formal employment exists only (or at least mainly) in the modern sector, and (*b*) that non-formal employment (which includes self-employment, casual wage employment and regular employment) exists principally in the traditional sector.

Two facts emerge quite clearly from the data for the year 1955 presented in Table 2.1. First, agriculture was almost wholly in the traditional sector; only 1 per cent of agricultural employment was formal (that was to be found in tea, coffee and rubber plantations). Second,

Table 2.1 Structure of employment in modern and traditional sectors, 1955

	X(1)		X(2)	
	Formal employment	Non-formal employment	Formal employment	Non-formal employment
Agriculture	1.1	98.9	11.8	82.9
Manufacturing	23.0	77.0	35.5	9.3
Construction	25.4	74.6	4.5	1.0
Other industries	79.2	20.8	5.5	0.1
Services	33.3	66.7	42.7	6.7
Total	7.3	92.7	100.0	100.0

Source: The estimates are derived from data cited in Mahalanobis (1958).

Note: X(1): share (percentage) in total employment in production sectors; X(2): share (percentage) in total employment in the economy. Other industries include 'mining and quarrying' and utilities (electricity, gas, and water).

though all the non-agricultural production sectors were dualistic, with modern and traditional segments, the modern sector of the economy was essentially non-agricultural, composed largely of manufacturing and services. Non-agriculture accounted for 88 per cent of formal employment in the economy (manufacturing and services together accounted for 78 per cent), while agriculture alone accounted for 83 per cent of non-formal employment in the economy.

Surplus labour, as noted above, exists in the form of underemployment of persons in self-employment and casual wage employment, which are the overwhelmingly dominant types of non-formal employment. Since most of the persons in non-formal employment were also in agriculture, it follows that much of the surplus labour also existed in agriculture. In other words, agriculture was the principal reservoir of surplus labour.

There was also a large gap in output per worker between agriculture and non-agriculture. In 1955, agriculture employed 78 per cent of the workers but produced only 52 per cent of the real output of the economy. This means that the average output per worker in non-agriculture was more than three times that in agriculture. It is to be expected that this large 'productivity gap' translated into a 'wage gap' between the two sectors, though empirical evidence on this is hard to find for the period under consideration.

It was also the case that very little capital was employed in agricultural production. This meant that capitalistic entrepreneurs existed basically in non-agriculture. The producers in agriculture were self-employed persons who employed mainly their own labour and land in production, which was meant to meet their own consumption requirements. Internally generated investment was basically absent in agriculture.

In the initial period of India's development, then, dualism could be defined in terms of agriculture and non-agriculture, agriculture corresponding to the traditional sector and non-agriculture corresponding to the modern sector. In other words, the traditional/modern dichotomy of the economy showed a high degree of correspondence to the agriculture/non-agriculture dichotomy. This correspondence survives in large measure to this day as we shall see in the following sections.

Judging Employment Trends

Assessment of time-trends in employment in a labour-surplus dual economy such as India's is made difficult by the fact that the standard indicators, such as change in the level of unemployment or growth in the number of persons in employment, that are normally used to make such assessment are not of much help.

As noted above, unemployment in this kind of an economy shows the extent of queuing for jobs in the modern sector by the 'young and educated' and not the extent of excess supply of labour in the economy as a whole. Any observed rise or decline in the rate of unemployment tells us, at best, something about changing degrees of mismatch between aspiration for and availability of jobs in the modern sector, but they tell us very little about improvement or deterioration in overall employment conditions. On the other hand, any observed change in the volume of employment (that is, in the number of persons in employment) also cannot tell us if employment conditions have improved or deteriorated since it does not tell us anything about changes in the level of underemployment and in the incidence of very low-productivity employment. Indeed, observed changes in employment tell us of little more than changes in the size of the labour force.

How then can we know if the employment conditions have been improving or deteriorating over time? The short answer is: (*a*) by assessing the extent of movement of employed persons from poor (that is, low-productivity) jobs to better (that is, more productive and remunerative) jobs, which usually means movement from jobs in the traditional sector or agriculture to jobs in the modern sector or non-agriculture; and (*b*) by tracking the change in labour productivity (output per worker) in the traditional sector or in agriculture.

In India's economy, four basic types of employment can be found: formal employment, regular employment, casual wage employment, and self-employment. In terms of quality, judged by the level of earning from work and/or by the per capita consumption expenditure of worker households, these four types of employment fall into a neat hierarchical order: formal employment is the best kind of employment, regular employment the second-best, self-employment the third-best, and casual employment the worst.[5] Obviously, then, improvement in overall employment conditions occurs whenever workers move from worse to better type of employment: from casual wage employment to any of the other types of employment; from self-employment to regular or formal employment; from regular employment to formal employment. Since formal and regular employment are the dominant forms of employment in the modern sector while casual and self-employment are the dominant forms of employment in the traditional sector, movement from jobs in the traditional sector to jobs in the modern sector unambiguously means movement from poorer to better jobs.

The nature of change in employment conditions is also indicated by the pattern of movement of workers across production sectors. Since the modern sector is basically non-agricultural and the traditional sector is roughly equivalent to agriculture, movement of workers from the traditional to the modern sector typically involves movement from agriculture to non-agriculture. However, movement from agriculture to non-agriculture does not unambiguously imply movement from the traditional sector to the modern sector because non-agriculture is dualistic in structure with traditional and modern segments. This does not matter much if it is the case that jobs in even traditional non-agriculture are better than jobs in traditional agriculture, which indeed is generally the case.[6] As discussed earlier, the average output per worker is much higher in non-agriculture than in agriculture so that movement from agriculture to non-agriculture usually means movement from less productive jobs to more productive and remunerative jobs. Such movement, therefore, generally imply improvement in overall employment conditions.

How can we know if movements of workers across different types of employment have been occurring? If each type of employment grows at the same rate, then total employment must also grow at this rate, and the share of each type of employment would remain unchanged through time. In this case, movement of workers from one type of employment to another can be said to be entirely missing. It is as if population growth results in a uniform rate of growth in the number of job seekers as well as in the number engaged in each type of employment. To put it another way, if the children of formal employees become formal employees themselves and the children of the self-employed become self-employed themselves and so on, and if population growth is exactly the same for each category of employed, the structure of employment will remain unchanged. For there to be movement of workers from one type of employment to another, the shares of different types of employment in total employment would have to change. If, for example, the share of formal employment in total employment is observed to have increased and the share of self-employment is observed to have correspondingly declined, it can be said that some workers have moved from self-employment to formal employment. Similarly, if the share of agriculture in total employment has declined while the share of manufacturing has increased, it can be said that some workers have moved from jobs in agriculture to jobs in manufacturing. Movement is indicated by unequal growth of different types of employment, that is, by change in the structure of employment by type or by production sector. Thus, change in the structure of employment is one important indicator of change in employment conditions.

A qualification needs to be added, however. Structural change unambiguously indicates movement of workers from one type of employment to another or from one production sector to another only when the total number of persons in employment is rising or at least constant. If this number is declining, structural change can occur without there being any movement of workers. The share of agriculture in total employment can decline, for example, if the number employed in it declines without there being any increase in the number employed in non-agriculture. Such situations do arise, if only rarely.

Growth of output per worker in the traditional sector is the other important indicator of change in employment conditions. When output per worker records positive growth, underemployment declines and earning from work increases for the self-employed and the casual wage-workers so that the quality of these types of employment improves. There are two factors that can contribute to growth of output per worker. The first is overall output growth in the traditional sector, which can happen when capital begins to be used in production (or, in other words, when there is investment in the traditional sector). The second is movement of workers out of the sector into jobs in the modern sector to such an extent that total employment in the traditional sector declines;

this increases output per worker of those who remain in the traditional sector even when output growth in the sector is zero. These two factors could of course also work together so long as the output per worker remains lower in the traditional sector; output growth in the traditional sector could be occurring while, simultaneously, some workers could be moving to jobs in the modern sector. Growth of output per worker in the traditional sector would naturally be more rapid in this case. In each of these situations, workers in the traditional sector effectively move to better jobs while actually remaining in the same jobs. A self-employed farmer, for example, effectively moves to a better job when irrigation makes land more productive (so that labour productivity rises and underemployment also declines) and/or when a working member of the farm household moves to a job outside the farm (so that underemployment of the remaining workers declines and hence the output per worker increases).

It should be evident from what has been said in the preceding discussion that output per worker in agriculture can serve as a good proxy for growth of output per worker in the traditional sector. This is important because empirical evidence on output per worker in agriculture is far more easily available than that on output per worker in the traditional sector.

That an increase in output per worker in the traditional sector or in agriculture translates into an increase in earnings from work for the self-employed is self-evident since the self-employed are both producers and workers. But it is not obvious why an increase in output per worker should also result in increased earnings from work for the casual workers. An explanation is required and this comes from an understanding of the method of determination of the daily wage for casual labour.

As already noted, the supply of casual labour is, indeed has to be, perennially in excess of its demand. This means that the casual wage cannot be determined through a demand–supply equilibrium since no such equilibrium can ever exist. How then is it determined? Here it is important to recognize that the casual wage workers and the self-employed (at least the large bottom layer of the self-employed) do not constitute non-overlapping categories. The same household often has one member working as self-employed and another working as casual wage worker. Many of the self-employed also work as casual wage workers for a part of the time, just as many of the casual wage workers also work as self-employed for a part of the time. In general, self-employment is the fall-back position for casual wage workers and casual wage work is the fall-back position for the self-employed. Labour-income per workday from self-employment, therefore, sets the norm for daily wage of casual workers. However, casual workers face uncertainty of employment, which the self-employed do not. An individual casual worker cannot expect to find work on all days he/she seeks it and cannot know in advance the number of days for which he/she will be in employment in a given period; the daily wage has to be a little higher than labour-income per workday from self-employment to compensate for this. Labour-income per workday from self-employment, it should be noted, is a fraction of total income per workday from self-employment, for, total income from self-employment is composed of rental income, profit-income, and labour-income.

The implication of all this is that growth of casual wage is closely linked to growth of income from self-employment, which generally results from growth of output per worker in the traditional sector. In other words, growth of output per worker in the traditional sector increases labour-income per workday for the self-employed and thereby causes growth of casual wage. On the other hand, in the absence of any growth in output per worker, an increase in casual wage (for whatever reason) does not necessarily increase the earnings of casual workers. This is because the wage rise increases the gap between casual wage and labour-income per workday from self-employment, and the

31

increased gap induces some of the self-employed to seek casual employment. The result is an increasing the level of underemployment of casual workers. The effect of increased daily wage then gets largely or even entirely cancelled out by a decline in the number of days of employment. It is growth of output per worker in the traditional sector or in agriculture, not autonomous growth of the wage rate, that unambiguously indicates improvement in the quality of casual employment.

Economic Growth, Employment, and Development

Employment, it is clear, has two interrelated characteristics. On the one hand, it results in output of goods and services; human labour is a factor of production. On the other hand, it generates income, in the form of wages for the wage-employed and income from enterprises—mixed income that incorporates rent, profit, and wages—for the self-employed. Hence, employment constitutes the most important link between production and income. In the context of an economy, the state of employment conditions defines the relation between the level of production and the level of living of the mass of population. Similarly, the nature of association between growth of production and change in employment conditions defines the effect of production growth on the level of living of the population.

This is why employment is central to development, which means steady improvement in material conditions of life for the population. The extent to which economic growth brings about development critically depends on the extent to which economic growth improves employment conditions. For it is when the employment conditions improve that the level of living of the mass of population improves. It is because the association between economic growth and employment is not pre-determined or given that economic growth is not equivalent to economic development. Improvement in employment conditions cannot occur without economic growth. But economic growth does not necessarily and inevitably improve employment conditions. In other words, economic development without economic growth is impossible but economic growth without economic development is perfectly possible.

As discussed earlier, improvement in overall employment conditions in a labour-surplus dual economy such as India's requires (*a*) movement of workers from low-productivity jobs in the traditional sector (or agriculture) to high-productivity jobs in the modern sector (or non-agriculture) and (*b*) growth of output per worker in the traditional sector (or agriculture). These requirements define the kind of economic growth that improves employment conditions and thus brings about development. For one thing, growth of the modern sector has to be such as to engender employment growth that is faster than the labour force growth in the economy; this is required to generate movement of workers from the traditional to the modern sector. To put it in economists' language, the combination of rate of output growth and employment elasticity (the rate of change in employment in relation to the rate of change in output) in the modern sector has to be such as to generate a rate of employment growth that exceeds the given rate of labour force growth in the economy as a whole. For another, growth must not remain confined to the modern sector alone; there has to be significant output growth in the traditional sector as well. The only situation in which growth of the modern sector alone can improve overall employment conditions in the economy is when this growth generates employment growth rapid enough to make labour force growth in the traditional sector zero or negative. But this growth rate is simply too high to be achievable except when the growth of the labour force itself is very low or zero.

This perspective explains why growth without development remains an ever-present possibility in labour-surplus dual economies. Saving and investment occur essentially in the modern sector of such economies; the traditional sector lacks entrepreneurs who could save and invest. In the absence of active state initiative, therefore, growth tends to occur only in the modern sector. Even if the consequent growth of employment in the modern sector is higher than the labour force growth in the economy, which typically is high and often accelerating, growth in the number of workers in the traditional sector still remains quite high. The reason is that the modern sector employs only a small proportion of the labour force in the economy to begin with so that the rate of growth of employment in the sector has to be impossibly high if the absolute number of workers in the traditional sector is to remain unchanged or to decline. In the absence of state investment in the traditional sector, therefore, there is zero growth of output and hence there is a decline in output per worker in that sector, which means increased underemployment and lower earnings from work. Economic growth, then, does not bring about development because it gets associated with declining output per worker in the traditional sector, which means deteriorating employment conditions and increasing poverty.

It is important to understand why population growth in developing countries is typically high and often accelerating. The explanation lies in the phenomenon of demographic transition, which refers to the inverted U-shaped trajectory of population growth that has been observed in all countries of the world. At a low level of development, both the birth rate and the death rate are high so that population growth is low. With economic progress, population growth first accelerates (because the death rate declines while the birth rate remains unchanged at a high level), then stabilizes at a high level (because the birth rate also begins to decline and catch up with the death rate), then decelerates (when the birth rate declines faster than the death rate), and finally stabilizes at a low level (when both birth and death rates have fallen to low levels). Being late starters, many developing countries are only at the first stage of demographic transition (when population growth is accelerating), some are at the second stage (when population growth is stable but high), and a few are at the third stage (when population growth is decelerating). The developed countries reached the final stage of the transition a long time ago.[7]

It is perhaps not so surprising, then, that many developing countries have actually experienced growth without development. If growth with development is to be achieved, growth of the modern sector (or non-agriculture) has to be high, this growth has to be employment-intensive, and growth of the traditional sector (agriculture) has to be high enough to ensure significant growth of labour productivity (output per worker). These are not easy conditions to meet when population growth is high. But it must be said that awareness of the need to meet these conditions has also been missing. It is crucially important that this awareness is there and guides the formulation and implementation of growth strategies in developing countries.

Notes

1. Value added from such work cannot be directly measured and has to be thought of as equal to the 'wage' received by the person(s) engaged in this work. The only way of assigning a value to this 'wage' is to think of this as the cost of hiring a person for domestic or care work. But is it right to consider this as the value of the family member's work when she is engaged in the same activity?

2. The concept was developed by Lewis (1954). In general, a dual economy emerged under colonial rule when a 'capitalist economy' was established by the colonizers alongside the pre-existing 'native economy' of the colonized. Also, under colonial rule, a long period of overall economic stagnation combined with positive population growth to generate stocks of surplus labour in the 'native economy'.

3. The statistical data cited here are taken from Mahalanobis (1958).

4. The estimate of poverty incidence is taken from Datt (1998).

5. See Ghose (2016) for detailed analysis and evidence.
6. Direct evidence on this is provided in Ghose (2016).
7. See Ghose (2016) for more elaborate discussion and evidence.

3

Trends

In the mid-1950s, when India was preparing to embark on planned economic development, employment conditions in the country were very poor not because many people were unemployed but because most people were employed in low-productivity economic activities. Today, too, employment conditions are poor not because there is high unemployment but because there is high incidence of low-productivity employment. Unemployment and employment do not mean the same things in the context of India's economy that they do in the developed economies of the world. Assessment of employment trends, therefore, cannot be done by simply tracking the quantitative significance of unemployment and employment; it calls for a fairly complex analysis of movement of people from bad (that is, low-productivity) jobs to good (that is, higher-productivity) jobs.

This chapter first sketches the nature and characteristics of unemployment and employment in India to show why these cannot serve as useful indicators of employment conditions. It then goes on to assess whether and to what extent the employment conditions in the country have improved in the years since Independence. To this end, it examines the nature and extent of movement of workers from low-productivity jobs to higher-productivity jobs over time as also the trends in underemployment and earnings from work.

Box 3.1 Employment statistics

The statistical data on employment and unemployment, used in the study, have been derived mainly from: (*a*) various rounds of National Sample Survey of Employment and Unemployment conducted by the National Sample Survey Office (NSSO), Central Statistical Organisation, Ministry of Statistics and Programme Implementation, Government of India; (*b*) one round of the Annual Employment–Unemployment Survey conducted by the Labour Bureau, Ministry of Labour and Employment, Government of India; (*c*) the database on employment in what is called the organized sector maintained by the Directorate General

---

of Employment and Training (DGET), Ministry of Labour and Employment; and (*d*) the decennial population censuses. The NSSO survey, the principal source of employment statistics in India, began in 1955 and was conducted annually till the early 1970s, but the methodology was still evolving. The different rounds of the survey used different reference periods, sampling methods, and coverage so that the data were not strictly comparable. A standardized survey methodology was introduced in 1972/73 but the survey has been conducted once every five years since then. Exceptionally, however, one round was conducted in 2011–12. The Labour Bureau survey, which uses the same methodology as the NSSO survey, began much later, in 2011/12, but has been conducted annually. Quite naturally though, the first couple of rounds were somewhat like trial runs in nature. In light of all this, for purposes of description and analysis in this book, the data have been derived from 10 rounds of the NSSO survey (1955, 1972/73, 1977/78, 1983, 1987/88, 1993/94, 1999/2000, 2004/05, 2009/10 and 2011/12) and one round of Labour Bureau survey (2015/16).

Because the surveys typically underestimate population, the ratios and proportions from the surveys are combined with estimates of population from the censuses to derive the absolute numbers relating to

41

employment, unemployment, and so on. We have used the annual data on India's population (by age group) produced by the United Nations Population Division (World Population Prospects, 2017 Revision),[*] which are based on the data available from the decennial population censuses of India.

The NSSO and Labour Bureau surveys use several reference periods and thus several definitions of employed and unemployed persons. The particular definitions chosen for this study are the Usual Status definitions. Accordingly, an employed person is one who has been engaged in economically gainful activities for at least 30 days in the past year, and an unemployed person is one who has not been engaged in economically gainful activities even for 30 days in the past year but has been looking or available for such engagement. The base estimates of total population, adult population, labour force and employment used in this study are presented in Table 3.1 later.

It should be said that in India, the year of reference for statistical data is rarely the calendar year; it usually covers parts of two years rather than full calendar years. The NSSO surveys, for example, typically cover a period from July of calendar year 1 to June of calendar year 2. Thus, the years are mentioned as 1972/73, 1973/74, and so on rather than as 1972, 1973, 1974,

Table 3.1 Population, labour force, and employment in India (numbers in million)

	Population (15+)		Labour force (15+)		Employment (15+)	
	Female	Total	Female	Total	Female	Total
1955	121.3	250.7	47.3	167.5	47.1	165.5
1973	183.2	353.1	83.7	236.7	83.0	233.2
1978	208.5	401.8	98.6	268.9	94.4	261.4
1983	219.5	455.6	99.5	303.6	98.4	298.2
1988	266.2	514.3	114.8	335.7	111.9	327.3
1994	306.8	593.9	131.7	383.1	129.6	375.5
2000	354.2	687.3	136.2	420.3	133.7	410.1
2005	395.8	769.0	147.1	466.7	143.1	456.1
2012	428.6	883.6	137.9	490.3	134.6	479.9
2016	461.3	950.8	126.3	496.0	119.0	477.5

Source: Author's estimates.

Note: The data on population (15+) are taken from the UN Population Division database (see https://population.un.org/wpp/). They are for the years shown. The estimates of labour force and employment are derived by multiplying the labour force to population and employment to population ratios, available from Mahalanobis (1958) for 1955 and from the NSSO and Labour Bureau surveys for the other years, by the figures for population (15+).

and so on. The data on population, however, refer to calendar years. For our purposes, we assume the ratios and proportions from the employment surveys to be valid for the second of the calendar years involved (the figures for 1972/73 to be valid for 1973, for example). We use them together with data on population for the corresponding calendar years. We, therefore, refer to calendar years throughout the book.

Notes: * See https://population.un.org/wpp/.

Unemployment and Employment: Nature and Characteristics

The striking fact about the observed unemployment rate in India is that it has been low and also stable over quite a long period (Figure 3.1).[1] A developed economy with such low rates of unemployment would have been designated a full–employment economy. Moreover, the persistence of such low rates over such a long period in a developed economy would have been viewed as nothing short of a miracle. Yet, it would obviously be absurd to make these claims for the Indian economy, which, it is universally recognized, has a very serious employment problem.

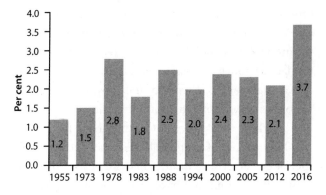

Figure 3.1 Rate of unemployment (%)

Source: Author's estimates based on data from Mahalanobis (1958), NSSO surveys, and Labour Bureau survey (see labourbureau.gov. in).

As a matter of fact, unemployment in India essentially reflects queuing by the educated youth from relatively well-off households for jobs in the modern sector and not the excess supply of labour in relation to demand in the economy as a whole (as it does in developed economies). The reason the unemployment rate is low is that only a small proportion of the fresh entrants into the labour force belongs to the category of 'educated youth'. The fact that it has been quite stable over time indicates that the queue of the 'educated youth' for jobs in the modern sector has not been getting longer over time. This does not necessarily imply that the growth of jobs in the modern sector has been keeping pace with the growth in the number of 'educated youth' entering the labour force. It means that after a certain period of waiting, many of them do find jobs in the modern sector, some opt for jobs in the traditional sector, and some perhaps even move out of the labour force.

Three pieces of empirical evidence underline the special characteristics of unemployment in India. One is that the unemployed have always been, and still are, far less poor and far more educated than the employed (see Table 3.2). While the incidence of poverty has been on the decline for all, it has always remained significantly higher for the employed than for the

Table 3.2 Poverty incidence and education level

	Percentage below poverty		Average years of education	
	Employed	Unemployed	Employed	Unemployed
1983	61.0	46.5	2.9	8.9
1999/00	46.4	33.2	4.3	10.1
2011/12	24.5	19.3	5.9	10.9

Source: Author's estimates based on data from NSSO surveys.
Note: The poverty lines used are Tendulkar Poverty Lines defined in Planning Commission, Government of India, *Report of the Expert Group to Review the Methodology for Estimation of Poverty*, 2009.

unemployed. While the level of education has been on the rise for all, it has always remained significantly lower for the employed than for the unemployed.

A second piece of evidence is that the rate of unemployment rises steadily with the level of education (Figure 3.2). At any given point of time, unemployment rate is insignificant for persons with up to primary education, moderate for persons with up to secondary education, high for persons with above secondary education and very high for persons with tertiary education. It will be noticed that the rate of unemployment for persons with tertiary education was higher in 2016 than in the other two years; this indeed

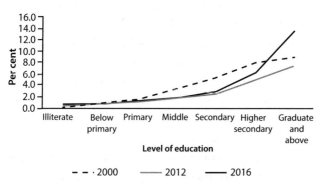

Figure 3.2 Unemployment rate (%) by level of education

Source: Author's estimates based on data from Mahalanobis (1958), NSSO surveys, and Labour Bureau survey.

is why the overall unemployment rate was also higher in 2016 than in the other two years (Figure 3.1). It is not clear if any particular significance is to be attached to this relatively high unemployment rate as it remains to be seen if this represents a random occurrence or a new trend. It should be said, however, that as the proportion of labour force entrants with at least secondary education rises, we can expect the overall unemployment rate to rise as well. But the data scrutinized here do not allow us to conclude that such a trend has already become visible.

A third piece of evidence is that for the educated, the unemployment rate is highest for the very young (fresh entrants into the labour force) and declines steadily and speedily with age; it becomes insignificant even for educated persons aged 30 years or more.[2] This suggests that after a certain period of waiting, most of the initially unemployed educated persons do find employment, though some of them possibly find it in the traditional sector and some opt out of the labour force.

Clearly, given these special characteristics of unemployment, rises or declines in the unemployment rate do not say much about the nature of change in overall employment conditions in the economy. But nor does the time-path of the other standard indicator—employment (that is, the number of persons in employment). This is because growth of employment in India's economy essentially reflects growth of the labour force (that is, supply of labour) and not growth of jobs (that is, demand for labour). An increase in the number of persons in the labour force means an increase in the number of persons in employment because unemployment is not an option for most people while the scope for work-sharing is wide. It is of little surprise that empirically, the rate of growth of employment is almost always found to equal the rate of growth of labour force (see Table 3.3).

Observed changes in the rate of growth of employment in the economy as a whole, therefore,

Table 3.3 Average annual growth (%) of population and employment

	Population	Population (15+)	Labour force	Employment
1955–73	2.1	1.9	1.9	1.9
1973–83	2.3	2.6	2.5	2.5
1983–94	2.1	2.4	2.1	2.1
1994–2000	1.9	2.5	1.5	1.5
2000–12	1.5	2.1	1.3	1.3
2012–16	1.2	1.9	0.3	−0.1

Source: Author's estimates based on data from the UN Population Division, Mahalanobis (1958), NSSO surveys, and Labour Bureau survey.

tell us very little about changes in employment conditions. A non-recognition of this fact has sometimes led to wrong diagnoses or unnecessary conundrums. The decelerating employment growth in the economy since the early 1990s, for example, has sometimes been taken to unambiguously indicate declining ability of economic growth to generate jobs when it may very well be reflecting nothing more than the deceleration in labour force growth. Some observers have even talked about 'jobless growth', which really is an impossibility in the context of the aggregate economy. Growth of jobs is nothing other than growth in the number of persons in employment, and so long as the number of persons in the labour force keeps growing, the number of persons in employment must also grow. In India's economy, therefore, employment actually grows quite independently of economic growth, which, of course, is never constrained by labour supply, which is plentiful. So, slow economic growth appears 'job-rich' while rapid economic growth appears 'jobless'. Neither of these appearances represents reality.

This said, it needs to be pointed out that observed changes in employment growth in the modern sector do tell us something about changes in overall employment conditions. For it is in the modern sector that employment growth actually reflects growth in the demand for labour. Employment growth in the traditional sector is in the nature of a residual; it is labour force growth net of employment growth in the modern sector. Decelerating employment growth in a context of stable or accelerating output growth in the modern sector does indeed indicate declining ability of economic growth to generate jobs. Jobless growth in the modern sector is perfectly possible. Decelerating employment growth in the modern sector also results in deteriorating employment conditions in the economy as a whole since it adversely affects the process of movement of workers from low-productivity to high-productivity jobs. For a given rate of labour force growth, a decelerating employment growth in the modern sector means an accelerating employment growth in the traditional sector, which would in general be associated with rising underemployment and lower earnings from work there. Similar observations can be made, though with somewhat lesser accuracy, about employment growth in non-agriculture (an imperfect proxy for the modern sector) and agriculture (an imperfect proxy for the traditional sector). Decelerating employment growth in a context of accelerating output growth in non-agriculture does indicate declining ability of economic growth to generate jobs and consequent worsening of employment conditions in agriculture.

The important fact is not that employment growth has been decelerating but that the labour force growth has been decelerating and a meaningful question that can and should be asked is why this has been so. The simple answer is that the labour force participation of the adult population has been declining since the early 1980s (Figure 3.3). Indeed, it declined rather sharply in recent periods; the total labour force grew at just 0.7 per cent per annum during 2005–12 and at an even lower 0.3 per cent per annum during 2012–16 while the adult population was growing at around 2 per cent per annum throughout 2005–16. To a very large extent, moreover, the declining labour force participation

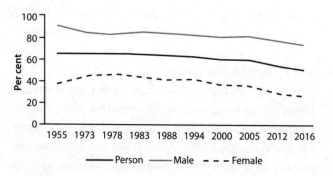

Figure 3.3 Labour force participation rate (%)

Sources: Author's estimates based on data from Mahalanobis (1958), NSSO surveys, and Labour Bureau survey.

of the adult population reflects the sharply declining labour force participation of adult females; this declined from 47 per cent in 1978 to 27 per cent in 2016. The decline has been particularly sharp in the period since 2005: from 37 per cent in 2005 to 27 per cent in 2016. In fact, the female labour force has been declining in absolute terms since 2005.

The main factors that lie behind the declining labour force participation of adult females has been identified through analysis.[3] One is that a growing proportion of them has been pursuing education. But this in fact explains only a very small part of the decline in their labour force participation; if the labour force participation rate is defined with reference to adult non-student population rather than to adult population, the rate still shows a sharply declining trend.[4] The much bigger part of the explanation is that a growing proportion of adult females with little or no education and largely from poorer households in rural areas has been withdrawing from the labour force. The reason is that the jobs they can find are of very poor quality, involving arduous work and poor earning.[5] While many women with little or no education had earlier been forced by extreme poverty to engage in these jobs (the phenomenon of distress participation), declining poverty (resulting in large part from rising earnings of adult males) made it possible for them to withdraw. At the same time, there is little doubt that availability of better jobs would have prevented their withdrawal from the labour force; withdrawal from poor jobs did not have to mean withdrawal from the labour force. The fact that the former meant the latter indicates that better jobs had remained unavailable. The declining participation of adult females, then, is explained by a combination of two factors: declining poverty and non-availability of jobs of acceptable quality.

One other noteworthy fact is that while the growth of total population was decelerating after 1983, the growth of adult population remained at a high level till 2005 and then began to decelerate (see Table 3.3). Also, throughout the period 1983–2016, the growth of adult population remained significantly higher than that of the total population. A more detailed picture is given by Figure 3.4, which shows that the population growth was accelerating till the early 1970s, remained stable at a high level till the mid-1980s, and then began to decelerate. The growth of adult population (aged 15 or more years) was accelerating till the mid-1970s, remained at a high level from the mid-1970s to the end of the century, and decelerated after 2000.

These patterns reflect the particular stages of demographic transition (a phenomenon that was discussed in Chapter 2) that India has been traversing:

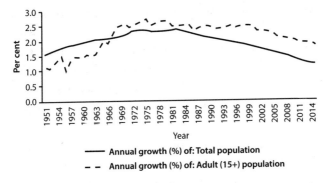

Figure 3.4 India's demographic transition

Source: The source of the data used to construct the figure is UN Population Division, which prepared the annual estimates of population by age group on the basis of the data generated by the decennial population censuses conducted by the Government of India.

the first phase of accelerating growth of population ended by the early 1970s, the second phase of stable but high growth ended by the late 1980s, and the third phase of decelerating growth is still ongoing. Each phase of demographic transition has naturally been associated with a particular kind of change in the age structure of the population: when population growth was accelerating, the share of children in total population was rising; when population growth remained stable but high, the share of working-age population was rising; and when population growth began to decelerate, the share of elderly population began to rise. There were some time lags involved, however. The share of children in total population kept rising for a period after population growth had stabilized, and the share of working-age population kept rising for a period after population growth began to decelerate.

One economic benefit that a country's demographic transition could conceivably deliver is what is called the demographic dividend. As population growth stabilizes and the share of adult population in total population rises, labour force growth should normally (that is, with stable or even mildly declining labour force participation rate) accelerate. To the extent that this translates into acceleration of employment growth, the dependency ratio—the number of persons that a worker is required to support—declines. The lower dependency ratio should, in turn, mean lower consumption–income ratio and hence higher saving–income ratio. Thus, an increase in the share of adult population in total population can conceivably have the effect of increasing the pace of economic growth, that is, of generating a growth dividend. On the one hand more workers are potentially available for employment, and on the other hand there also are more savings potentially available so that increased investment is possible.

We should note, however, that growth acceleration is only a possibility and not a certainty because investment need not increase just because more savings are potentially available. Increased investment has to occur autonomously if potential increases in employment and savings are to be converted into actual increases. In the context of a labour-surplus dual economy such as India's, an acceleration in labour force growth could mean an acceleration in employment growth even in the absence of increased investment. But this would mean increased underemployment and lower productivity so that no growth dividend need arise.

As it happens, the rising ratio of adult population to total population since the mid-1970s has actually been accompanied by a deceleration in labour force growth as the labour force participation of the adult population has been declining through much of this period. Instead of declining, the dependency ratio has in fact been increasing in the period since the mid-1970s. Demographic dividend has remained a chimera.

Employment Trends, 1955–2016—an Assessment

A central question we need to answer is: Have employment conditions been improving during

1955–2016 and, if yes, to what extent? To answer this question, as we know by now, we need to examine the intertemporal changes in the structure of employment (by type and by production sector) as also the time trends in output per worker, earning from work, and underemployment in the traditional sector (or agriculture). It is such a scrutiny that is undertaken in what follows.

Structure of Employment by Type

How has the structure of employment by type been evolving? A first fact is that the share of self-employment in total employment has been declining, which of course means that the share of wage employment in total employment has been increasing, fairly steadily throughout the period (Figure 3.5). Thus, there was significant movement of workers from self-employment to wage employment throughout the period. This is in accord with what is nearly an iron law, namely, that wage employment gains in importance in the course of economic growth.

A second fact is that during 1955–2000, the declining incidence of self-employment was associated with rising incidence of casual employment. This means that, as a rule, workers were moving from self-employment to casual wage employment and

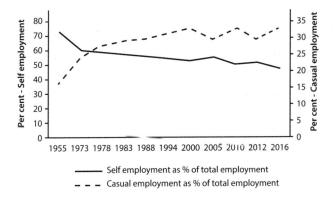

Figure 3.5 Self-employment and casual wage employment

Sources of data: Author's estimates based on data from Mahalanobis (1958), NSSO surveys, and Labour Bureau survey.

not to regular wage employment. There were two exceptions to this rule. During 2000–5, there seems to have been some movement from casual wage employment to self-employment and during 2005–12, there was some movement from self-employment to regular wage employment (since the share of casual employment remained stable even while the share of self-employment declined). During 2012–16, there was, once again, movement from self-employment to casual wage employment.

A third fact is that the share of formal employment in total employment showed significant increase only in two periods: 1955–73 and 2005–12; it declined between 1978 and 2005 and again between 2012 and 2016 (Figure 3.6). Thus, substantial movement of workers from non-formal to formal employment occurred only in two periods: 1955–73 and 2005–12. During 1978–2005 and again during 2012–16, the incremental workforce went largely into non-formal employment.

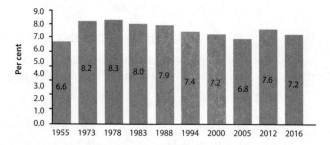

Figure 3.6 Formal employment as percentage of total employment

Sources: Author's estimates based on data from Mahalanobis (1958), NSSO surveys, and Labour Bureau survey.

Box 3.2 Data on formal employment

The DGET has been collecting data on employment in what is called the organized sector (defined to include all government and public sector establishments, all private corporate sector establishments and all private non-corporate establishments employing at least 10 workers) since the mid-1950s. More recently, four rounds of NSSO surveys (those for the years 2000, 2005, 2010, and 2012) have generated data on different types of employment in different types of establishments making derivation of estimates of different types of employment in the organized sector for those years possible. A comparison of the estimates derived from the two sources for the common years (2000, 2005, 2010, and 2012) tells us that the data collected by the DGET are best interpreted as data on formal employment and not as data on total employment in the organized sector. Based on this finding, the data series on formal employment used here is constructed by combining the DGET estimates for the years 1955, 1973, 1978, 1983, and 1994 with the estimates derived from NSSO data for the years 2000, 2005, and 2012. To this has been added an estimate of formal employment for the year 2016 derived from the Labour Bureau survey of that year, which also provides data on different types of employment in the economy.

Thus far, nothing has been said about movement of workers from the traditional sector to the modern sector. The reason is that available empirical evidence is much too limited to allow observation of trends over the entire period. It is true that nearly all formal jobs have been and are in the modern sector. But not all jobs in the modern sector have been or are formal; non-formal employment (that is, regular and casual employment) in the modern sector has for long been

---

Box 3.3 Empirical definitions of the modern sector

The modern sector corresponds to what in India is called the organized sector, the generally accepted definition for which is that given by the DGET (see Box 3.2) and we use this definition in much of the analysis. However, in national accounts statistics, the organized sector is defined in this way only in the case of manufacturing; for the other production sectors, the organized sector includes only the government, the public sector, and the private corporate sector establishments. As it happens, the NSSO surveys allow the flexibility of deriving estimates of employment in the modern sector by using either of the definitions. So, whenever we need to combine employment and output data for analysis, we use the definition used in national accounts statistics. The traditional sector is always taken to be a residual category, that is, the non-modern part of the economy.

---

substantial and growing. So, the time trend in the share of the modern sector in total employment cannot be inferred from the observed time trend in the share of formal employment in total employment.

Detailed statistical data on employment in the modern sector is available only for the period 2000–12 (see Table 3.4). Two interesting facts emerge

Table 3.4 Employment in the modern sector

	2000	2005	2010	2012
Formal employment in the modern sector as % of total employment in the economy	7.2	6.8	7.3	7.6
Total employment in the modern sector as % of total employment in the economy	11.7	12.8	15.3	17.5
Share (%) of formal employment in total employment in the modern sector	62.4	56.6	49.6	44.7

Source: Author's estimates based on data available from NSSO surveys.

Note: Here, the modern sector (which, in India, is referred to as the organized sector) is defined to include all government, public sector, and private corporate sector establishments, and private non-corporate sector establishments with 10 or more employees.

from these data. First, much of the employment in the modern sector has been and is non-formal. Already in 2000 the share of non-formal employment in modern sector employment was as high as 38 per cent, and it kept increasing in the years that followed. Second, during the same period, while the share of formal employment in total employment showed only a small increase (from 7.2 per cent to 7.6 per cent), the share of the modern sector in total employment showed a large increase (from 12 per cent to 17 per cent). During 2000–5, while the share of formal employment in total employment actually showed a decline, the share of the modern sector in total employment still showed an increase. These facts confirm that the unobserved trend in the share of the modern sector in total employment cannot be inferred from the observed trend in the share of formal employment in total employment.

The remarkable fact that formal employment share in the modern sector was already as low as 62 per cent in 2000 strongly suggests that this share had begun to decline long before 2000 (since it can be plausibly supposed that formal employment share in the modern sector was close to 100 per cent at the beginning, that is, in the 1950s). A reasonable guess is that within the modern sector, non-formal employment had started to grow faster than formal employment after 1978, when the growth of formal employment began to steadily decelerate. Thus, it is likely that even though the share of formal employment in total employment in the economy was declining during 1978–2005, the share of the modern sector in total employment was still rising through this period as well. This means that throughout the period 1978–2005, there was movement of workers from non-formal employment in the traditional sector to non-formal employment in the modern sector.

The overall picture emerging from a review of structural change by type of employment, then, is as follows (see Box 3.4). During the period 1955–78, overall employment conditions recorded negligible change. There was significant movement from non-formal jobs in the traditional sector to formal jobs in the modern sector, which indicates substantial gains in productivity and incomes. At the same time, however, there also was significant movement from self-employment to casual wage employment, which suggests worsening employment conditions within the traditional sector. Overall, employment conditions in the economy can thus be said to have deteriorated somewhat (given that the traditional sector employed most of the workers). During 1978–2000, overall employment conditions showed a more significant deterioration. The share of formal employment in total employment was declining so that there was little movement of workers from non-formal to formal jobs. Some workers moved from non-formal jobs in the traditional sector to non-formal jobs in the modern sector and this indicates very modest gains in productivity and incomes. On the other hand, some workers also moved from self-employment to casual employment and this suggests a deterioration in the quality of employment in the traditional sector. On balance, employment conditions can be said to have deteriorated to a certain extent. It was during 2000–12 that overall employment conditions showed significant improvement. There was movement of workers from non-formal jobs to formal jobs, from non-formal jobs in the traditional sector to non-formal jobs in the modern sector, and from self-employment to regular employment. So, there was quite significant movement from low-quality to higher-quality jobs. During 2012–16, employment conditions showed signs of deterioration. There was no movement from non-formal to formal employment and some movement from self-employment to casual employment. When viewed over the entire period (1955–2016), the striking fact that emerges is that the average quality of employment in the economy hardly changed at all (see Box 3.4).

Box 3.4 Employment quality index

In any given period, employment conditions can show improvement in one respect and deterioration in another respect. For example, the formal employment share and the casual employment share (in total employment) can both increase simultaneously; the former indicates improvement while the latter indicates deterioration. The nature of change in employment conditions then becomes ambiguous. It is possible to develop a clearer view by constructing an employment quality index (EQI)* as follows. We can assign numbers to indicate the quality ranking of each type of employment (discussed in Chapter 2): formal employment, 4; regular employment, 3; self-employment, 2; and casual employment, 1. Then, for any given year, we can derive a value of EQI as a weighted average rank: [(formal employment share × 4) + (regular employment share × 3) + (self-employment share × 2) + (casual employment share × 1)] / 100.

The estimates derived for the relevant years are: 1955, 2.021; 1978, 1.943; 2000, 1.893; 2012, 1.972; 2016, 1.939. It is then easy to see that the average quality of employment showed deterioration during 1955–2000, improvement during 2000–12, and deterioration during 2012–16. It is also clear that over the entire period of

1955–2016, the average quality of employment showed a slight deterioration, if anything.

*Such an index was developed in Ghose (2016).

Structure of Employment by Production Sector

The first fact to note is that the share of agriculture in total employment declined throughout the period, though the decline was rather insignificant during 2012–16. So, at least during much of the period, workers were moving out of jobs in agriculture into jobs in non–agriculture (Figure 3.7). This is very much in accord with the nearly iron law that the importance

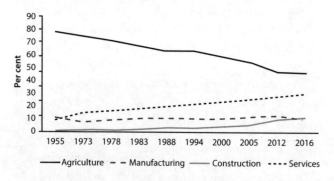

Figure 3.7 Share (%) in total employment

Sources: Author's estimates based on data from Mahalanobis (1958), NSSO surveys, and Labour Bureau survey.

of agriculture as a job-provider declines in the course of economic growth. This change typically improves overall employment conditions since jobs in non-agriculture are typically better (more productive and remunerative) than jobs in agriculture.

What is remarkable, however, is that the pace of decline in agriculture's share was rather slow even during 1955–2012. This becomes clear when we compare the pace of decline in India with that in some Asian countries. Between 1965 and 2010, the share declined from 74 per cent to 51 per cent in India, while it declined from 82 per cent to 37 per cent in China, from 57 per cent to 7 per cent in Korea, from 45 per cent to 5 per cent in Taiwan, and from 80 per cent to 38 per cent in Thailand.[6] Moreover, even the slow decline in the employment share of agriculture in India is explained in part by factors that are unrelated to the growth process and in fact indicate the failure of the growth process to generate jobs in non-agriculture. One is the declining labour force participation of women; most of those withdrawing from the labour force were withdrawing from casual wage employment in agriculture; this contributed to the decline in agriculture's share in total employment. The other is job creation in construction through special employment schemes (as we shall see below); this contributed to the rise in non-agriculture's share in total employment. Thus, growth-induced structural change in employment was even slower than the observed structural change.

A second fact is that throughout the period 1955–2016, the share of manufacturing in total employment in the economy barely changed; it fluctuated around a mean of 11 per cent. So, manufacturing was not a significant employer of the workers moving out of agriculture. This in fact explains why the movement from agriculture to non-agriculture has been slow; the employment share of agriculture is observed to have declined rapidly in precisely the countries where the employment share of manufacturing increased steadily. The share of manufacturing in total employment, for example, showed rapid increase in the successful developers of Asia: from 8 per cent in 1970 to 19 per cent in 2010 in China; from 8 per cent in 1963 to 28 per cent in 1988 in Korea; from 13 per cent in 1963 to 34 per cent in 1987 in Taiwan; and from 5 per cent in 1970 to 15 per cent in 2007 in Thailand.[7] As we have seen, these were also the economies in which the share of agriculture in total employment declined far more rapidly than in India. Indeed, in economic history, remote and recent, as countries began to develop, workers moved from agriculture to both manufacturing and services, but primarily to manufacturing at initial stages and primarily to services at later more developed stages. The reason is that manufacturing led the growth process at early stages of development and services became the lead sector only at late stages. In India, workers have been moving from agriculture to services but not to manufacturing at a rather early stage of development. India's growth process too is being led by services at a rather early stage of development as we shall see.

A third fact relates to the apparently important role of construction in absorbing workers moving out of agriculture. This again stands in contrast with what has been observed in other Asian countries; the share of construction in total employment in India is much higher than what it is in other more advanced developing countries of Asia. In 2010, the share of construction in total employment was 12 per cent in India, 8 per cent in China, Korea, and Taiwan, and 6 per cent in Thailand.[8] Strikingly, the share of construction in total employment in India's economy began to increase in the late 1970s and increased particularly sharply from 2005 onward. By 2016, construction had become a more important employer than manufacturing. These trends underline the importance of some particular government interventions—the special employment schemes[9] and certain rural development programmes[10]—in India's economy. These schemes and programmes were

71

designed to generate mainly casual wage employment in construction, and their implementation had been rendered necessary by the failure of the growth process to generate non-agricultural jobs at a rapid enough pace. The trends perhaps also underline the role of remittances, a significant part of which went into construction of housing and real estate, particularly in rural areas. The inflow of remittances, it may be noted, began to grow rapidly in the early 1990s, and its growth was particularly rapid during 2005–12.

A fourth fact is that the share of formal employment in total non-agricultural employment increased during 1955–73 but declined steadily thereafter (Figure 3.8).

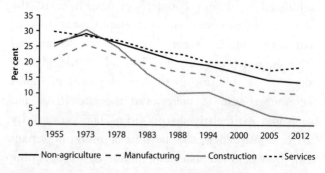

Figure 3.8 Share (%) of formal employment in total employment

Sources: Author's estimates based on data from Mahalanobis (1958), NSSO surveys, and Labour Bureau survey.

Moreover, while the decline in formal employment share occurred in all non-agricultural sectors during 1973–2005, it was truly dramatic in construction, where it had declined from 31 per cent in 1973 to 3 per cent in 2005. Moreover, the formal employment share of construction continued to decline after 2005, while it remained stable in the case of manufacturing and increased in the case of services. Quite strikingly, formality of employment in construction had actually increased between 1955 and 1973, indicating that construction in this period was associated mainly with investment. At any rate, it is quite clear that throughout the period 1973–2005, workers were moving out of employment in agriculture into non-formal employment in non-agriculture. This evidence provides further confirmation of three trends already identified above, namely, (*a*) that significant growth of non-formal employment in the modern sector commenced in the late 1970s; (*b*) that during 1978–2005, there was significant movement of workers from non-formal employment in the traditional sector to non-formal employment in the modern sector; and (*c*) that during 2005–12, workers moved from non-formal employment in the traditional sector to both formal and non-formal employment in the modern sector.

The overall picture emerging from a scrutiny of structural change by sector, then, is as follows. The pace of movement of workers out of agriculture has been rather slow throughout the period considered. This is attributable to the fact that manufacturing has not been a significant employer of the workers moving out of agriculture, who could find employment basically in services and in construction. Employment growth in construction, however, had much to do with the implementation of special employment schemes and rural development programmes by the government, and indicates the failure of the growth process to generate rapid growth of jobs in modern manufacturing and services. Moreover, for much of the period, the new jobs in non-agriculture were non-formal; formal jobs in non-agriculture recorded decent growth only during 1955–73 and again during 2005–12.[11] In terms of structural change, overall employment conditions improved somewhat during 1955–73, when the movement of workers from agriculture to non-agriculture was relatively slow but involved movement from non-formal to formal jobs, and again during 2005–12, when the movement from agriculture to non-agriculture was relatively rapid but involved movement from non-formal to formal jobs. During 1973–2005, employment conditions recorded only slight improvement on account of structural change as the growth of formal employment in non-agriculture was low and decelerating, and workers moved basically from non-formal employment in agriculture to non-formal employment in non-agriculture. During 2012–16, there was little movement of workers from agriculture to non-agriculture, which suggests deterioration of overall employment conditions.

Output per Worker in the Traditional Sector

In the context of India's economy, as already pointed out, time trend in output per worker in the traditional sector is the most important indicator of the nature of change in employment conditions within that sector. It is growth of output per worker that raises labour incomes and reduces underemployment of both self-employed and casual workers.

Given the nature of data availability, something can be said about the time trend in output per worker in the traditional sector only for the period 1983–2012. It is possible, however, to examine the time trend in output per worker in agriculture, which is a good proxy for output per worker in the traditional sector, for the period 1955–2012. Though some estimates of output per worker for the period 2012–16 can be derived, these are not strictly comparable to those for the period up to 2012. For there was a change of base year (from 2004–5 to 2011–12) for the national accounts data, which made the output data for the period after 2012 non-comparable to those for the period up to 2012.[12]

Real output per worker in agriculture recorded negligible growth during 1955–83, moderate growth during 1983–2000, and rapid growth during 2000–12 (see Table 3.5). Real output per worker in the traditional sector also showed moderate growth during 1983–2000 and rapid growth during 2000–12. Both indicators, reassuringly, show very similar trends. Noticeably, throughout 1983–2012, the real output per worker in the traditional sector increased faster than that in agriculture. The reason obviously is that the growth of output per worker was faster in traditional non-agriculture than in agriculture.

Close associations among output per worker, real wage of casual labour, and real income from self-employment are also quite evident. The real wage per day in casual employment in agriculture, the lowest wage in the economy, increased at a moderate rate during 1983–2000 and at a rapid rate during 2000–12. The growth of real mixed income per self-employed was very similar to that of real wage of casual labour in both periods. Sketchy evidence available for the period 2012–16 suggests stagnation of real wage in agriculture.[13] For lack of data, we cannot know precisely how wages and incomes had changed during 1955–83. However, given that output per worker in

Table 3.5 Average annual rate of growth (%)

	1955–78	1955–83	1978–2000	1983–2000	2000–12
Agriculture					
Real output per worker	0.5	0.5	1.6	2.1	3.6
Real daily wage of casual labour				2.0	5.0
Real annual mixed income per self-employed				3.0	2.2
Traditional sector					
Real output per worker (1)					5.4
Real output per worker (2)				2.6	5.5
Real daily wage of casual labour					5.1
Real annual mixed income per self-employed				3.1	5.1

Source: Author's estimates based on data available from NSSO surveys for employment and from Central Statistics Office (National Accounts Statistics) for output.

Note: For output, the deflator is GDP deflator; for wage and mixed income, the deflator is the consumer price index for agricultural labourers. For the traditional sector, real output per worker (1) is defined as the ratio of real net domestic product (NDP) to total employment for the traditional sector; real output per worker (2) is defined as the ratio of unorganized sector's real NDP to total number of self-employed and casual workers in the economy. For agriculture, real output per worker is defined as the ratio of real agricultural GDP to total employment in agriculture.

agriculture recorded negligible growth during this period, it can be safely deduced that both the real wage of casual labour and the real income from self-employment recorded negligible growth.[14]

How did the level of underemployment change during 1955–2016? Depending upon data availability, three different indicators can be used to study the trend in underemployment: the rate of underemployment of casual workers (days of unemployment as per cent of the days offered for employment in a specified period), the rate of non-employment (days/months not worked as per cent of days/months available in a specified period) of casual workers, and the rate of non-employment for all workers in the economy. Since underemployment basically affects the casual workers and the self-employed (that is, the workers in the traditional sector), an estimate of underemployment of all workers in the economy is naturally an underestimate of underemployment of workers in the traditional sector. But it is reasonable to expect the two indicators to move in the same direction.

The estimates show that underemployment tended to decline when output per worker in agriculture (traditional sector) increased (see Table 3.6). The rate of underemployment showed a generally declining trend during 1955–2012, but the decline was significant only for the period 1983–2012. For the period 1955–83,

Table 3.6 Underemployment

	Casual wage workers		All workers
	Rate (%) of underemployment	Days not worked as % of days available	Days/months not worked as % of days/ months available
1955			15.6
1983	16.7	27.9	14.1
2000	11.3	21.1	11.4
2012	8.9	17.0	7.6
2016			13.5

Source: Author's estimates. For the years 1983, 2005, and 2012, the estimates are based on data from the NSSO surveys. For 1955, the estimates are based on data from Mahalanobis (1958). For 2016, the estimate is based on data from the Labour Bureau survey for that year.

Note: Rate of underemployment is the number of days of unemployment expressed as percentage of the number of days offered for employment in a week. In estimating the other two indicators, days available are taken to be the total days available (seven days in a week, for example) and not the days offered for employment. The estimate for 1955 shows the days not worked as per cent of days available for employment in a 30-day period. The estimate for 2016 shows the number of months not worked as per cent of months available in a year.

the rate of non-employment of all workers showed only a slight decline suggesting insignificant change in underemployment. For the period 1983–2012, there is more solid evidence. The average rate of underemployment for casual workers, the workers who face the most serious underemployment, declined throughout the period 1983–2012. For this period, the trends suggested by the other two indicators—the rate of non-employment of casual workers and the rate of non-employment for all workers—are the same: underemployment declined steadily during 1983–2012. For the period 2012–16, the evidence, though rather sketchy, suggests rising underemployment; the rate of non-employment for all workers shows a fairly sharp increase during the period.

The picture that emerges is as follows: Employment conditions in agriculture (traditional sector) showed little improvement during 1955-1983, some improvement during 1983–2000, substantive improvement during 2000–12 and some worsening during 2012–16. Remarkably, during 1983–2000, when structural change was slow and there was significant movement of workers from self-employment to casual employment within agriculture (traditional sector), employment conditions in the sector still improved because of significant growth of output per worker, which increased labour incomes and reduced underemployment. During 2000–12, faster structural change combined with faster growth of output per worker to bring about substantial increases in labour incomes together with significant reduction in underemployment in agriculture (traditional sector). A slowdown in structural change as also in growth of output per worker led to a worsening of employment conditions in agriculture (traditional sector) during 2012–16.

A Tour d'Horizon

The three indicators of employment trends paint a very consistent picture. They show that there were four clearly identifiable phases of evolution of employment conditions in India over the period 1955–2016.

During 1955–78 (phase 1), formal employment grew faster than the workforce, which meant that some workers moved from non-formal to formal employment and thus from the traditional to the modern sector. At the same time, some workers moved from self-employment to casual wage employment within the traditional sector. The average quality of employment in the economy deteriorated, as the estimated values of the EQI (Box 3.4) show.

Movement of labour from (low-productivity) agriculture to (higher-productivity) non-agriculture was slow. Output per worker in agriculture recorded negligible growth. So, earning from work did not grow and underemployment did not decline. In short, employment conditions improved for some—those who moved from agricultural employment to non-agricultural employment—but remained at best unchanged for a large majority of the workers who continued to work in the traditional sector. Overall, employment conditions cannot be said to have improved.

During 1978–2000 (phase 2), formal employment grew at a slower rate than the workforce, which, of course, meant that non-formal employment grew faster than the workforce. Thus, the incremental workforce went primarily into non-formal employment (basically self-employment and casual wage employment). Some workers moved from non-formal employment in the traditional sector to non-formal employment in the modern sector, which was growing faster than formal employment. The structural change in employment was in the wrong direction, showing deterioration in conditions; the estimated values of the EQI show this quite clearly (Box 3.4).

However, output per worker in agriculture recorded significant growth, and employment conditions in the traditional sector improved on this account. Earning per unit of work for the self-employed and the casual workers recorded significant growth. Underemployment also declined, so that total earnings from work for these workers increased faster than earning per unit of work. Thus, overall employment conditions in the economy improved significantly even though the structural change was unfavourable and the quality of employment in the modern sector worsened since the share of formal employment in total employment declined. A qualification needs to be added, however. The growth of employment in construction was quite rapid during the period and this is attributable, to a significant extent, to the special employment and rural development schemes that were implemented nationwide from the late 1970s onward. But for these, the movement of workers from agriculture to non-agriculture would have been slower and the improvement in overall employment conditions would have been somewhat smaller.

During 2000–12 (phase 3), formal employment again grew faster than the workforce; some workers moved from non-formal employment to formal employment. Within the modern sector, however, non-formal employment increased much faster than formal employment. By the end of the period, non-formal employment had actually become predominant in the modern sector. Clearly, while some workers moved from non-formal employment to formal employment, many more moved from non-formal employment in the traditional sector to non-formal employment in the modern sector. On the whole, the structural change in employment was in the right direction—the value of the EQI increased (Box 3.4)—suggesting improvement in employment conditions.

Moreover, employment conditions within the traditional sector improved very substantially. Output per worker in agriculture as also in the traditional sector grew rapidly. So, earning per unit of work increased rapidly for the casual workers and the self-employed. Underemployment also declined very substantially so that earning from work for the self-employed and the casual workers increased even faster than earning per unit of work. Overall, employment conditions improved substantially even though the quality of employment in the modern sector declined once again.

However, there was a flip side to all this: the labour force participation rate declined quite sharply during this period basically because of a sharp decline in the labour force participation of women; consequently, the growth of the labour force was slow (just 1.3 per cent per annum) even though the growth of the adult population remained high (at 2.1 per cent per annum). This fact lowers the significance of improvement in employment conditions during the period. Had labour force participation not declined so sharply, labour force growth would obviously have been significantly higher and improvement in employment conditions would thus have been less impressive. Moreover, the decline in the participation rate itself reflected, to a certain extent, non-availability of decent jobs for poorer and less educated women, particularly in rural India. On the whole, the improvement in employment conditions during the period was real but not as substantial as it appears at first.

It is also to be remembered that very rapid growth of employment in construction played an important role in pulling labour out of agriculture into non-agriculture during this period and this growth is attributable in large measure to the special employment schemes and rural development programmes implemented by the government. In the absence of these programmes, too, the improvement in employment conditions would have been less impressive.

During 2012–16 (phase 4), employment conditions appear to have deteriorated. The growth of formal employment was negative and so was the growth of total employment. The share of formal employment in total employment declined. Output per worker in agriculture does seem to have recorded some growth. Yet, inexplicably, the real wage of casual labour in agriculture seems to have stagnated and underemployment appears to have increased. So, the growth in total earnings from work could not have been very significant for the self-employed and the casual workers. Moreover, labour force participation declined for both men and women, more sharply for women, so that the growth of labour force itself was negligible. This too points to deteriorating employment conditions.

When viewed over the entire period of 1955–2016, the inescapable conclusion is that while the employment conditions in India certainly improved, the extent of improvement has been surprisingly small. Remarkably, moreover, even the small improvement came more from growth of output per worker in the traditional sector than from structural change in employment. Formal employment certainly did not grow in importance and non-formal employment came to predominate even in the modern sector of the economy. From being dualistic, construction became transformed into a traditional sector like agriculture. Even in 2016, self-employment and casual employment together still accounted for 80 per cent of total employment in the economy, and agriculture and construction together accounted for nearly 60 per cent.

A few striking features of the process of evolution of employment conditions deserve to be highlighted. The *first* is India's non-industrialization; the failure of manufacturing to generate rapid employment growth is a basic cause of the slow pace of structural change and hence in overall employment conditions over such a long period. The *second* is the rising importance of non-formal employment in the modern sector. This facilitated movement of workers from the traditional to the modern sector both because it stimulated employment growth in the modern sector (the fact that non-formal employees cost less than formal employees had a stimulating effect on the demand for labour in the modern sector) and because it allowed employment of relatively low-skilled workers (who gained by moving from non-formal employment in the traditional sector to non-formal employment in the modern sector). But at the same time, of course, it lowered the average quality of jobs in the modern sector. The *third* is the growth of formal employment being largely confined to services, a fact we have not had occasion to mention thus far. The share of services in total formal employment in the economy increased from 43 per cent in 1955 to 73 per cent in 2012. Much of the formal employment in services, moreover, has been in government establishments and public enterprises; in 2012, about 74 per cent of formal employment in services was in the public sector. The private sector, it seems, has not been creating many 'good' jobs. The *fourth* is the rapid growth of non-formal (mainly casual) employment in construction during

1983–2012, but for which the movement of workers from agriculture to non–agriculture would have been slower than it actually was. The average annual growth of employment in construction was 3.6 per cent during 1955–78, 6.7 per cent during 1978–2000, and 8.8 per cent during 2000–12. The share of casual employment in total employment in construction was 69 per cent in 2000 and increased to 84 per cent in 2012. The average annual growth of employment in construction slumped to 2.2 per cent during 2012–16 but still remained impressive in a context where total employment in the economy appears to have actually declined in absolute terms.

Finally, there is the fact of downward trend in labour force participation of adult (aged 15 years or more) women since the early 1980s, precisely the period when India might have been in a position to reap a demographic dividend. Women's labour force participation has now fallen to a distressingly low level.[15] As stated above, analysis suggests that the growing pursuit of education explains only a very small part of the sharp decline in labour force participation of adult females since the mid-1990s. The principal explanation is to be found in the withdrawal of rural women from 'distress participation'. The withdrawal, of course, was made possible by the declining incidence of poverty, but it also was caused by declining opportunities for employment. This is because withdrawal from 'distress participation' did not have to mean withdrawal from the labour force; it could have meant movement from very poor jobs to better jobs. The fact that withdrawal from 'distress participation' actually meant withdrawal from the labour force suggests the non-availability of decent jobs.

Notes

1. The figure for 2016 seems exceptionally high and we can only view this as an outlier at this point.
2. A detailed scrutiny of this evidence is available in Ghose (2016).
3. See Ghose (2016).
4. A growing proportion of adult males has also been pursuing education and this fully explains their mildly declining labour force participation.
5. Remarkably, most of the women who withdrew from the labour force had previously been engaged in casual wage employment in agriculture.
6. The estimates for countries other than India are based on data available from the 10-sector database maintained by the Groningen Growth and Development Centre, University of Groningen (Netherlands). See https://www.rug.nl/ggdc/.
7. Based on data available from the 10-sector database maintained by the Groningen Growth and Development Centre.

8. Based on data available from the 10-sector database maintained by the Groningen Growth and Development Centre.

9. Special employment schemes have been implemented in rural India since the late 1970s. The most important of such schemes—the Mahatma Gandhi National Rural Employment Guarantee Scheme (MGNREGS)—was launched in 2005. Under this scheme, 100 days of employment at a stipulated minimum daily wage is to be provided on demand to rural workers. Jobs generated under the scheme have very largely been in construction activities.

10. Examples are special programmes for construction of rural roads and rural housing.

11. The average annual rate of growth of formal jobs in non-agriculture was 3.3 per cent during 1955–78, 1.4 per cent during 1978–2005, and 2.4 per cent during 2005–12. The corresponding growth rates of total employment in non-agriculture were 3.2 per cent, 3.8 per cent, and 2.9 per cent respectively.

12. Though national accounts data, estimated by using 2011/12 as the base year, for a few years prior to 2011/12 have now been made available, their reliability remains open to doubt.

13. See Himanshu (2017).

14. There is some evidence to suggest that between 1961 and 1969, real mixed income per self-employed in the economy (not just in agriculture) fluctuated without showing any trend, and recorded very slow growth (0.2

per cent per annum) between 1970 and 1975. See Sen (1991).

15. For the year 2010, the female labour force participation rate was 29 per cent in India, 64 per cent in China, 51 per cent in Indonesia, 49 per cent in Korea, 47 per cent in Malaysia, and 64 per cent in Thailand. (The data for countries other than India are taken from World Bank's *World Development Indicators 2018*; see https://datacatalog.worldbank.org/dataset/world-development-indicators.)

4

Economic Growth and Employment

Employment conditions in India, as the analysis in the preceding chapter has shown, have improved too little over too long a period, mainly because the pace of structural change in employment has been far too slow. On the other hand, India's growth performance has been far from poor, as we shall see in the following sections. This suggests a disconnect between economic growth and employment. How did such a disconnect arise? This is the question we seek to address in this chapter.

Three distinct phases stand out in India's growth story during the period since Independence. The first phase, lasting from the mid-1950s till the late 1970s, was when the economy was quasi-closed and the Nehru–Mahalanobis strategy of state-led industrialization prevailed. The second phase, lasting from the late 1970s till the early 1990s, was when state participation was rolled back from the economy, private entrepreneurs were accorded enhanced roles, and imports were liberalized to a limited extent. The third and ongoing phase began in 1993 when, in response to the economic crisis of 1992, India's quasi-closed economy was opened up to trade and capital flows. Each of these phases was associated with growth acceleration.

The effect of economic growth on employment structure was of course not exactly the same in these different phases of growth. However, except perhaps in the first phase when growth itself was relatively slow, the effect was weak and grew weaker over time. Growth accelerations did not bring commensurate accelerations in the pace of structural change in employment.

Why this was so is the question that this chapter seeks to address. It first sketches with a broad brush the shifts in the pace and pattern of growth during 1955–2016 and then takes a view of how and why economic growth affected employment in the way it did.

The Pace and Pattern of Economic Growth, 1955–2016

In the mid-1950s, development planners in India formulated a strategy of growth, often referred to as the Nehru–Mahalanobis growth strategy, which sought to promote rapid economic growth through state-led industrialization, with a strong emphasis on heavy industries manufacturing capital and intermediate goods, under a protective trade regime.[1] At the time, when trade pessimism was a widely shared view among development economists, the strategy seemed quite sensible, particularly for a large country. India's economy, however, grew at a disappointing 3.5 per cent per annum between 1955 and 1978, roughly the lifespan of this growth strategy. On this account, the Nehru–Mahalanobis growth strategy is often judged to have been a failure. But it needs to be recognized that the relatively slow rate of economic growth, often derided as the 'Hindu rate of growth', was actually much faster than what had been achieved during the final half-century of British colonial rule. It is also good to remember that the period 1955–78 witnessed three wars, two episodes of severe drought, and the first 'oil price shock', all of which were unforeseen events that had serious disruptive effects on economic growth. When all this is kept in view, the growth rate of 3.5 per cent does not seem all that unimpressive.

The policy regime began to change in the early 1980s when the Nehru–Mahalanobis growth strategy was effectively abandoned.[2] Partial liberalization of the domestic economy loosened state control and

94

accorded greater importance to market forces and the private sector. There also was some liberalization of imports, particularly of capital goods imports. Growth accelerated to about 5 per cent in the early 1980s and the economy continued to grow at this rate till the early 1990s. Through the 1980s, however, fiscal expansion and external borrowing were relied upon to sustain this higher growth, which continued to be based on import substitution. Fiscal expansion sustained the growth of domestic demand while external borrowing was used to finance growing imports of capital goods embodying newer technologies that sustained growth of domestic production through faster growth of productivity. The import–GDP ratio increased from 6.3 per cent in 1978 to 9.6 per cent in 1991. The export–GDP ratio, in contrast, barely moved—it increased from 6.1 per cent in 1978 to 7 per cent in 1991. The inevitable result was growing trade deficit and accumulation of external debt, which eventually led to a serious economic crisis in 1991.

In responding to the crisis, the government implemented a series of economic reforms that opened up India's hitherto quasi-closed economy to external trade and capital flows. After just one year of low growth, the economy, having received fresh stimulus from trade expansion and foreign investment, returned to a higher growth of 6 per cent per annum, which was sustained till the early 2000s. However, availability of foreign finance remained critical to sustaining the high growth during this period as well since trade deficit continued to be high at 2.4 per cent of GDP on average. But the source of foreign finance had changed from external borrowing to foreign investment and remittances from Indians working abroad.

Surging exports of information technology–related services, increasing inflow of remittances and growing inflow of foreign capital triggered another growth acceleration in 2004. During the period 2003–12, growth averaged more than 8 per cent in spite of the shock delivered by the global financial crisis of 2009. However, this period of high growth also witnessed rapidly increasing trade deficit, which reflected the increasing import intensity of consumption, investment, and even exports. The large and growing inflows of foreign finance and remittances helped sustain this large and growing trade deficit, which reached over 6 per cent of GDP in 2012. In effect, the high growth was being sustained by large and growing inflows of foreign finance and remittances in this period of high global liquidity and growth. The inflow of foreign finance increased from around 2 per cent of GDP in 2003 to around 4 per cent in 2012. Remittances constituted over 3 per cent of GDP through the period from 2004 to 2012.

That sustainability of high growth had become contingent on sustainability of high trade deficit and hence on sustainability of large inflows of foreign finance became clear when, after 2012, there was growth deceleration. We need to be careful here. For there are problems of comparability of national accounts data for the period up to 2012 with that for the period after 2012.[3] But the observation that there was growth deceleration after 2012 is most unlikely to be wrong even though the question of the degree of deceleration must remain open.[4] The important point is that growth deceleration in the post-2012 period cannot be attributed to any change of policy regime, which in fact remained substantially unchanged. What changed were the magnitudes of inflows of foreign finance and of remittances, which declined. The inflow of foreign finance declined from 3.5 per cent of GDP in 2012 to 1.6 per cent in 2017. Remittances also declined from 3.5 per cent of GDP in 2012 to 2.5 per cent in 2017. Trade deficit had to decline and it did, from 6.9 per cent of GDP in 2012 to 1.9 per cent in 2017. This naturally involved a squeeze on imports, which adversely affected investment and exports, given their import dependence. Between 2012 and 2017, the import–GDP ratio declined from 31.7 per cent to 21.3 per cent; the export–GDP ratio declined from 24.8 per cent to 19.4 per cent; and the investment rate declined from 34.3 per cent to 28.2 per cent.

The battery of statistics cited above establishes two rather simple points. First, even if it is granted that India's growth performance was unimpressive during 1955–78, it certainly was not so during 1978–2012, when growth averaged over 6 per cent per annum. Though less rapid than the growth achieved by China and some other East Asian countries, India's growth has still been quite impressive. Second, India's growth strategy changed in a rather peculiar way in the early 1980s when the Nehru–Mahalanobis strategy was abandoned. The new strategy was not one of export-oriented industrialization, a strategy that had enabled the East Asian economies including China to achieve very rapid transformation of their economies. Rather, it was a strategy of growth propelled by foreign finance. The reforms of the early 1990s did not alter this growth strategy; they actually consolidated it.

The pattern of growth had also changed in the early 1980s and did not really change again. During 1955–78, manufacturing had led the growth process. In the early 1980s, services became the lead sector. Through the subsequent reforms and growth accelerations, the lead role of services in the growth process only got strengthened. This too stands out as rather peculiar because there is no other instance in remote or recent history of services-led growth in an economy at such an early stage of development (see Box 4.1).

Box 4.1 The enigma of India's services-led growth

Historically, in all successful developers, which include today's developed countries as well as the late developers of Asia—Japan, Korea, Taiwan, and China—growth was led by manufacturing at early stages of development. Economists[*] have explained this by pointing to four special characteristics of manufacturing: increasing returns to scale in manufacturing production,[**] high tradability of products, high income elasticity of demand[#] for manufactures at low levels of income, and the ability of manufacturing to employ low-skilled workers at a productivity premium. The traditional characteristics of services stand in sharp contrast: constant returns to scale in production,[§] non-tradability of products, low income elasticity of demand at low levels of income, and inability to employ low-skilled workers at a productivity premium.

How, then, is India's services-led growth at a rather early stage of development to be explained? Some economists[^] have argued that in the twenty-first century, services-led growth has become as feasible as manufacturing-led growth even at early stages of development. This is because, so the argument runs, recent technological developments, particularly the advances in digital technology, have transformed certain services, which have now acquired at least two of the traditional characteristics of manufacturing, namely, increasing returns to scale in production and high tradability of products. The most prominent examples of such services are IT services.

That such developments have occurred cannot be denied. But the argument that such services can lead the growth process in developing countries just as well as manufacturing is far from convincing. The services that have acquired some of the characteristics of manufacturing typically account for a tiny part of the national output in developing economies. Even in India, after years of rapid growth, the IT services—the only services that India has been a net exporter of—accounted for less than 6 per cent of services output and just over 3 per cent of GDP in 2012. With such small weight in output, these services can hardly be the engine that pulls the economy at much more than a snail's pace.

As a matter of fact, India has witnessed rapid growth of all services and not just of the services transformed by digital technology. Moreover, this growth has been led by domestic demand and not by exports. What needs to be explained is the rapid growth of domestic demand for services in a low-income economy such as India's. The only sensible explanation is that incomes of the rich (whose consumption bundle includes more services than goods) have grown much faster than incomes of the rest. To explain India's premature services-led growth, we need to understand why and how incremental incomes have largely accrued to the rich. This is where the role of foreign finance shows up to have been prominent.

★ These characteristics were identified by Kaldor (1967) and came to be known as Kaldor's Growth Laws.

★★ Increasing returns to scale exist when a doubling of inputs more than doubles the output.

Income elasticity of demand is the rate at which demand increases when income increases by one per cent.

§ Returns to scale are constant when a doubling of inputs just doubles the output.

^ See, for example, Dasgupta and Singh (2007).

In truth, India's services-led growth has actually been foreign finance–led growth. It has been a growth process in which inflows of foreign finance have generated incomes for the already rich, which in turn have generated demand for services as also for high-end manufactures, the production and distribution of which, being skill-intensive activities, have also generated incomes for the relatively rich. It is not accidental that income inequality, which had shown a declining trend till the early 1980s, has shown a sharply rising trend since then. The income share of the top 1 per cent of the Indians increased sharply, from 6 per cent in 1983 to 22 per cent in 2014.[5] Services-led growth has clearly gone hand in hand with growth of income inequality. And, contrary to a common presumption, the rapid growth of services in India has been domestic demand–led and not export-led.[6] Manufacturing meanwhile has not just lagged behind but has also been shifting to import-intensive production, even mere assembly, of high-end goods, the demand for which was also being driven by the growing income inequality.[7] The combined effect of the shift of domestic production toward services and the shift of manufacturing toward import-intensive production of high-end goods has been rapidly rising deficit in merchandise trade and thus rising overall trade deficit. Inflows of foreign finance has been sustaining the rising trade deficit, thus completing the circle. A triad of foreign finance inflow, income inequality, and trade deficit has remained hidden behind India's 'exceptional' services-led growth.

This is no place to pursue the growth story any further. What matters is the fact that since the early 1980s, the pace of economic growth has been quite impressive and the question that concerns us here is why this impressive growth did not bring impressive improvement in employment conditions.

Economic Growth and Employment

How does economic growth affect employment? In the context of India's economy, to recall earlier discussions, economic growth can improve employment conditions through two channels: (*a*) by generating movement of workers from low-productivity jobs in the traditional sector to higher-productivity jobs in the modern sector, thereby changing the structure of employment; and (*b*) by engendering growth of output per worker in the traditional sector, thereby improving the quality of jobs there. Overall economic growth is composed of growth of the modern sector and growth of the traditional sector. Growth of the modern sector— the lead sector in the economy—generates new higher-productivity jobs and pulls workers out of the traditional sector to take up these jobs. In other words, growth of the modern sector brings about structural change in employment. Growth of the traditional sector, by increasing the productivity of the workers who continue to work in the sector, improves the quality of the already existing jobs by increasing labour incomes and reducing underemployment.

What emerges from the discussion in Chapter 3 is that the second of these processes worked reasonably well except during 1955–78 when output per worker in the traditional sector (agriculture) recorded near-zero growth. But the pace of structural change in employment has been slow throughout the period 1955–2016, and this is the main reason why the improvement in overall employment conditions has been rather small. The question is why fairly rapid economic growth has been associated with such a slow pace of structural change in employment.

Empirical investigation into the issue encounters certain difficulties posed by problems of data availability. Statistical data relating to output in modern and traditional sectors are available for the period 1981–2012 while data relating to employment in the sectors are available only for the period 2000–12. Data on output in modern and traditional sectors for post-2012 years are available but, as already pointed out, there are serious problems of comparability of these with the data for pre-2012 years.[8]

Under the circumstances, the period of analysis must perforce be limited to 1955–2012, and agriculture and non-agriculture, for which data on both output and employment are available for the entire period, have to serve as imperfect but acceptable proxies for traditional and modern sectors respectively. As already noted, however, a significant part of the employment in construction has been generated through special employment programmes implemented by the government since the late 1970s and this effectively de-linked employment growth from output growth in the sector. This de-linking shows up in the fact that, from the late 1970s onwards, employment growth in construction has been high and accelerating while productivity growth has been negative or negligible (see Table 4.1). In light of this, it is appropriate to consider non-agriculture excluding construction as the proxy for the modern sector in analysing the

Table 4.1 Growth (% per annum) of output and employment

	Output			Employment		
	1955–78	1978–2000	2000–12	1955–78	1978–2000	2000–12
Non-agriculture	*4.6*	*6.0*	*8.4*	*3.2*	*3.6*	*3.6*
Construction	4.9	4.4	9.1	3.6	6.7	8.8
Non-agriculture excluding construction	*4.6*	*6.2*	*8.4*	*3.1*	*3.4*	*2.7*
Manufacturing	4.9	5.5	8.1	1.4	2.7	2.5
Services	*4.4*	*6.4*	*8.7*	*4.5*	*3.7*	*2.8*

Source: Author's estimates based on data from National Accounts Statistics and NSSO surveys.

effects of growth on employment. Non-agriculture, thus defined, is composed essentially of manufacturing and services, other industries (mining and utilities) constituting a very small component.

It is analytically convenient to make the phases of growth coincide with the phases of change in employment conditions identified in the last chapter since this can be done without introducing serious distortions into the growth story. When the periods 1978–91 and 1993–2000 are merged into a single period of 1978–2000, only the fact of slightly faster growth in the second part of the period gets ignored. And when the period 2000–12 is considered in place of the period 2003–12, nothing of substance gets ignored.

We can observe, to begin with, that the higher non-agricultural growth during 1978–2000 was not associated with commensurably higher employment growth in non-agriculture, and the second growth acceleration during 2000–12 was actually associated with a fairly sharp deceleration in employment growth (Table 4.1). To put it in the language of economics, the employment elasticity of non-agricultural growth—the rate of growth of employment associated with one per cent growth of output—declined between periods and particularly sharply between 1978–2000 and 2000–12 (see Box 4.2 and Figure 4.1). So, except during the first period, when economic growth itself was weak, the main factor behind the weak effect of economic growth on structural change in employment was the declining employment elasticity of non-agricultural growth. Therefore, precisely why the employment elasticity was declining is the central question that needs to be answered.

Box 4.2 Employment elasticity

Employment elasticity is the rate at which employment grows when output grows by 1 per cent. Empirically, this can be estimated as a ratio:

$$\eta = r(E) / r(Q)$$

where η is the employment elasticity, $r(E)$ is the average annual growth of employment during a certain period, and $r(Q)$ is the average annual rate of growth of output during the same period. In general, output growth can be thought of as deriving partly from employment growth and partly from growth of labour productivity (that is, output per worker):

$$r(Q) = r(E) + r(p)$$

where $r(p)$ is the average annual rate of growth of labour productivity. A little manipulation gives us:

$$\eta = r(E) / r(Q) = 1 - [r(p) / r(Q)].$$

From this it is easy to deduce the following:

- Since, in general, output growth results in part from employment growth and in part from productivity growth, $r(p) < r(Q)$ so that the employment elasticity is usually found to be somewhere between 0 and 1.
- If, in any given period, output growth results entirely from labour productivity growth, that is, if $r(p) = r(Q)$, the employment elasticity is zero.
- If, in any given period, output growth results entirely from employment growth, that is, if $r(p) = 0$, the employment elasticity is unity.
- As it is possible for productivity growth to be higher than output growth in a given period, it is possible for the employment elasticity to be negative (because $r(p)/r(Q) > 1$).

The above-mentioned equation also shows that employment elasticity declines when the ratio $r(p)/r(Q)$ increases (when acceleration of productivity growth is greater than acceleration of output growth or deceleration of productivity growth is smaller than deceleration of output growth) and increases when the ratio declines (when acceleration of productivity growth is smaller than acceleration of output growth or deceleration of productivity growth is greater than deceleration of output growth).

Why Was the Employment Elasticity of Growth in Non-agriculture Excluding Construction Declining?

Since non-agriculture excluding construction is composed essentially of manufacturing and services, a change in the employment elasticity of the sector's growth can be expected to result from a combination of (*a*) a change in the employment elasticity of manufacturing growth, (*b*) a change in the employment elasticity of services growth, and (*c*) changes in the relative shares of the two sub-sectors in total non-agricultural output. What we can observe straightaway is that the time trend in employment elasticity in manufacturing was different from that in services; the former first increased and then declined while the latter declined quite steadily (see Figure 4.1). The share of manufacturing in non-agricultural output also first increased and then declined; manufacturing-led growth of the first period was followed by services-led growth in the subsequent periods. However, services accounted for a very large share of non-agricultural output, 67 per cent at its lowest, throughout the period 1955–2012. So, the declining employment elasticity of non-agricultural growth reflected to a large extent the declining employment elasticity of services growth. Nevertheless, we need to take a deeper look at the

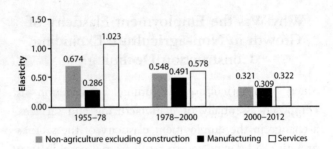

Figure 4.1 Employment elasticity

Source: Author's estimates based on data from the NSSO surveys and National Accounts Statistics.

distinctive trajectories of employment elasticity in manufacturing and in services in order to gain a proper understanding of the pace and pattern of employment growth in non-agriculture.

Employment Intensity of Manufacturing

The employment elasticity of manufacturing growth was low during 1955–78, high during 1978–2000, and then again low during 2000–12 (though still higher than that during 1955–78). The low employment elasticity of the first period is perhaps not all that surprising in view of the fact that growth of manufacturing in this period came basically from growth of heavy industries, which were capital-intensive in character. Growth of output, therefore, came more from growth of labour productivity than from growth of employment. Indeed, Mahalanobis, the principal architect of the Nehru–Mahalanobis growth strategy, had fully anticipated the weak employment effect of heavy industry–led industrialization and had proposed simultaneous development of small-scale industries for employment generation.[9]

But what explains the impressive increase in the employment elasticity in the second period? A rise in employment elasticity implies a fall in the ratio of productivity growth to output growth, that is, a larger acceleration of output growth than of productivity growth (see Box 4.2). As a matter of fact, productivity growth was slower and output growth faster during 1978–2000 than during 1955–78 (see Table 4.1). This itself, we may note, comes as something of a surprise; manufacturing is normally characterized by increasing returns to scale so that higher output growth is expected to be associated with higher productivity growth. So, what brought about a slowdown in labour productivity growth? The answer is to be found in two particular policy measures that were introduced in the 1970s.

The first was a piece of labour regulation that provided near-full job security to the workers employed in large-scale enterprises in the modern sector. An amendment to the Industrial Disputes Act of 1947, introduced in 1976, made it mandatory for enterprises employing 300 or more workers to seek authorization from the government for laying off formal employees or for closing down an establishment. Another amendment, introduced in 1984, widened the ambit of the provision to cover all enterprises employing 100 or more workers. The twice-amended Industrial Disputes Act made it very difficult for large-scale enterprises in the modern sector to adjust the size of their formal workforce essentially because the government found it very difficult to authorize lay-offs or closure. The amended regulation, therefore, effectively discouraged recruitment of formal employees and encouraged hiring of non-formal employees who were paid lower wages and could be easily dismissed. Since hiring of non-formal employees had the effect of lowering the average cost of labour, it also naturally stimulated employment growth in large-scale enterprises, particularly in private large-scale enterprises. Growth of modern manufacturing was thus associated with growth of non-formal employment of relatively low-skilled, low-wage workers. Between 1978 and 2000, the growth of formal employment in manufacturing was virtually zero. And by 2000, the share of non-formal employees in all employees in modern manufacturing was 56 per cent.

The second piece of policy measure was that of reservation of products for manufacture in small-scale industries in the traditional sector, which used highly labour-intensive methods of production. Though the need for such a policy had been recognized much earlier, it was put in place only in the late 1960s. The objective here was faster creation of jobs in manufacturing. To begin with, in 1967, 47 items were reserved for production exclusively by small-scale industries. But the number of reserved items increased very quickly; it climbed to 807 by 1978 and then to a peak of 872 by 1983. Through the period 1983–2000, the number remained somewhere between 812 and 850. Alongside product reservation, small-scale industries were also offered a variety of support through provisions of cheap credit, tax exemptions and government purchase programmes.[10] These policies naturally led to a significant expansion of small-scale industrial enterprises producing the reserved items. The average scale of production in the manufacturing sector as a whole declined as a result.

The combined effect of these two developments was an acceleration in employment growth together with a slowdown in labour productivity growth in manufacturing.

Why did the employment elasticity then decline so radically in the next period? The answer, it would seem, lies in a policy reversal. Following the liberalizing reforms of the early 1990s, a process of de-reservation of products for small-scale industries had begun but the process gathered steam only from around 2004. The number of reserved products declined from 842 in 1993 to 812 in 2001, then to 605 in 2004, then to 239 in 2007, and finally to just 20 in 2011. A process of withdrawal of the government support programmes naturally accompanied the process of de-reservation. Decline in the number of small-scale enterprises, now faced with competition not just from domestic large-scale industries but also from imports, was the result, and this meant a deceleration in employment growth and an acceleration in productivity growth in manufacturing.

This story receives support from the empirical evidence on growth of modern and traditional manufacturing available for the period 2000–12. This evidence shows that the employment elasticity of growth of modern manufacturing was in fact quite high in this period while that of traditional manufacturing was low (see Figure 4.2).[11] The high employment elasticity in the modern sector seems to have been associated with continued rapid growth of non-formal employment. Between 2000 and 2012, 89 per cent of the incremental employment in modern manufacturing was non-formal. The share of non-formal employment in total employment in modern manufacturing increased from 56 per cent in 2000 to 68 per cent in 2012.

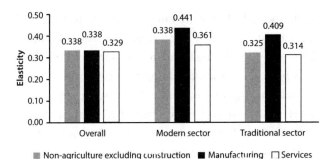

Figure 4.2 Employment elasticity, 2000–12

Source: Author's estimates based on data from the NSSO surveys and National Accounts Statistics.

The lower employment elasticity of traditional manufacturing, on the other hand, can be made sense of only if we can suppose that many of the small-scale manufacturing units, which had been set up in response to the strong incentives generated by the policy of product reservation and government support, were inefficient and did not survive de-reservation and withdrawal of government support and those that survived had done so by increasing labour productivity. New small-scale manufacturing units with higher labour productivity may also have competed out many of the old units with lower labour productivity. Thus, it was productivity growth, not output growth, in traditional manufacturing that showed an acceleration in the post–2000 period. Output growth in traditional manufacturing was 4.4 per cent per annum during 2000–12, scarcely higher than that during 1983–2000 (3.8 per cent per annum). Output growth in modern manufacturing, on the other hand, recorded a large acceleration, from 5.8 per cent per annum during 1983–2000 to 9.3 per cent per annum during 2000–12.

It is worth pointing out that certain widely held ideas about why job creation in modern manufacturing has been poor do not receive much support from the available empirical evidence. In the first place, of course, job creation in modern manufacturing cannot be said to have been particularly poor in the period since 1978. What is true is that growth of formal jobs has been very poor. The jobs created in this period have been very largely non-formal and thus of poorer quality. Second, the oft-repeated argument that capital-intensive industries within modern manufacturing have grown faster than labour-intensive industries in recent periods is factually incorrect; there is evidence to show that the labour-intensive industries have grown as fast as the capital-intensive industries.[12] What really has happened is that capital intensity has increased in both types of industries. Third, another oft-repeated argument that the Industrial Disputes Act severely constrained employment growth in modern manufacturing misses the point. In fact, it severely constrained growth of formal employment and stimulated growth of non-formal employment; the overall effect actually was accelerated employment growth.

Employment Elasticity of Services

The employment elasticity of services growth was high—slightly larger than unity—during 1955–78, the period of manufacturing-led growth. This implies that the growth of labour productivity was negative, as indeed it was. This need not be viewed as something very unusual; in historical experience, services growth is found to have been highly employment-intensive, at least at early stages of development when manufacturing led the growth process.[13] It is perhaps not without significance that 1955–78 was the only period when India had experienced manufacturing-led growth. Essentially, growth of manufacturing stimulates growth of certain kinds of services (trade and transport in particular) through a demand effect and these services are known to be employment-intensive.

Strikingly, the employment elasticity of services growth declined sharply during 1978–2000 and again during 2000–12, both of which were periods of services-led growth. Given that both of these periods witnessed accelerations in output growth, the implication is that the acceleration in labour productivity growth was larger than that in output growth in both periods. What explains such large accelerations in labour productivity growth?

The answer lies in the changing composition of services that the services-led growth was associated with. Sub-sectors of services fall into fairly neat categories in terms of employment intensity. The conventional services such as 'trade', 'hotels and restaurants', and 'transport and storage' are employment-intensive. So are the social services, which include 'public administration and defence', 'community and social services' (which include education and health services), and 'personal services'. On the other hand, the dynamic services such as 'communication services', 'financial services', and 'business services' (which include IT services as the major component), the services that have led the growth process since the early 1980s, are skill intensive and have very low employment intensity. Then there are 'real estate and renting services' which are the least employment-intensive of all services.

In 1955, the conventional and social services together accounted for 71 per cent of services output, the dynamic services for 5 per cent, and 'real estate and renting' for the remaining 24 per cent (Table 4.2). In 1978, these shares were, respectively, 75 per cent, 8 per cent, and 17 per cent. So, during 1955–78,

Table 4.2 Shares (%) of different types of services in total output and employment in services

	1955	1978	1983	2000	2012
Real output					
Trade, hotels, and restaurants	28.0	26.2	25.6	24.7	28.0
Transport and storage	9.6	13.7	14.6	12.7	11.6
Communication, financial and business	5.0	8.6	9.2	17.5	30.4
Real estate and renting	23.8	16.7	16.5	14.3	7.9
Community, social and personal	33.6	34.8	34.1	30.8	22.1
All services	100.0	100.0	100.0	100.0	100.0
Employment					
Trade, hotels, and restaurants			39.0	43.2	42.8
Transport and storage			13.3	14.4	15.1
Communication, financial and business			5.0	6.0	10.1
Real estate and renting			0.2	0.5	1.2
Community, social and personal			42.5	35.9	30.8
All services			100.0	100.0	100.0

Source: Author's estimates based on data from National Accounts Statistics and NSSO surveys.

the employment-intensive services were not just overwhelmingly dominant but also grew faster. This explains why employment growth in services exceeded output growth so that productivity growth was negative and the employment elasticity was slightly greater than unity.

After 1978, however, the pattern of growth changed; the skill-intensive dynamic services recorded much faster growth than the employment-intensive conventional and social services. Between 1978 and 2000, the combined share of conventional and social services in total services output declined from 75 per cent to 68 per cent, while the share of dynamic services increased from 9 per cent to 17 per cent. This pattern of change continued during 2000–12, only the pace of change was faster; the combined share of conventional and social services declined to 62 per cent while the share of dynamic services increased to 30 per cent. The explanation for the declining employment elasticity in both periods lies in the fact that employment-intensive conventional services grew at a slower pace than low-employment-intensity dynamic services.

★★★

The basic reason for the slow improvement in employment conditions in India is to be found in the failure of growth to bring about rapid enough structural change in employment. Except during 1955–78, when economic growth itself was slow, the explanation for the slow pace of structural change lay in sharply declining employment elasticity of non-agricultural growth. In the period since the late 1970s, the high and accelerating non-agricultural growth was associated with low and decelerating growth of non-agricultural employment. The non-agricultural sector, therefore, was pulling labour out of agriculture at a progressively slower pace. But for the withdrawal of women from the labour force, which largely meant withdrawal from agricultural employment, and the special employment schemes, which generated substantial employment in construction, the pace of structural change in employment would have been even slower than it has been.

There were two main factors behind the failure of non-agricultural growth to bring about structural change in employment at a rapid pace. The first relates to the failure of manufacturing to play its proper role in non-agricultural growth. Except during 1955–78, manufacturing has not had a lead role in the growth process. Non-industrialization—some would say de-industrialization—has been a prominent feature of India's growth experience. The share of manufacturing in non-agricultural output has actually been declining since the mid-1980s. The basic strengths of manufacturing—increasing returns to scale in production (which has a stimulating effect on economy-wide growth) and the ability to generate employment for low-skilled labour at a productivity premium—remained unrealized potentials. It must be said that these had remained unrealized potentials even during the early period of manufacturing-led growth because the emphasis placed on heavy industries ruled out the possibility of employment of low-skilled labour at a productivity premium, and the closed economy framework adopted ruled out the possibility of realization of scale economies.

The second factor relates to the bias against labour use that the services growth incorporated. Viewed in the context of international experience, the employment intensity of services in India stands out as being surprisingly low. In most countries, developed and developing, the share of services in total employment tends to equal their share in GDP.[14] In India, the share of services in employment tends to be far lower than their share in GDP; in 2012, the employment share was 28 per cent while the GDP share was 57 per cent. The services that have been leading the growth process— communication and financial and business services— are skill-intensive and make little use of low-skilled labour. Yet, it is not accidental that these services have had the lead role in the growth process. This is because these are the services that arguably have acquired some of the characteristics such as increasing returns to scale and tradability that had earlier been particular to manufacturing, enabling them to play the lead role in the growth process at early stages of development. When manufacturing led the growth process, services growth was employment-intensive because growth stimulus was generated for conventional and social services. In a services-led growth regime, services growth acquired a bias against job generation because the skill-intensive dynamic services held sway. Moreover, the growing income inequality associated with services-led growth led to growth of demand not just for services but also for modern versions of traditional services (shopping malls and e-commerce in retail trade, for example); this too had the effect of lowering the employment intensity (and of increasing the skill intensity) of services.

Notes

1. The growth model underlying the strategy was articulated in Mahalanobis (1955a).
2. Good accounts of India's changing growth strategies are available in: Rodrik and Subramanian (2005), Kochar et al. (2006), and Kotwal, Ramaswami, and Wadhwa (2011).

3. A new series of National Accounts Statistics, using a new base and new methods of estimation, are available for the period after 2012. Unfortunately, there are serious problems of comparability of the old and new series.

4. Estimates of comparable data for the period 1993/94–2017/18 have been made available (National Statistical Commission, Government of India, *Report of the Committee on Real Sector Statistics*, 2018), but these have not received official approval. A different set of officially approved estimates of comparable data for a much shorter period (2004/05–2017/18) has become available but usability of these data has remained open to question.

5. See Chancel and Piketty (2017).

6. See Ghose (2015) for analysis and evidence.

7. See Ghose (2016).

8. The data on output in modern (organized) and traditional (unorganized) sectors come from National Accounts Statistics. The problem of comparability of National Accounts Statistics for the period up to 2012 with those for the post-2012 period has been commented upon in note 3 of this chapter.

9. The idea was development of small-scale industries, which were labour-intensive, for production of consumer goods, while large-scale industries produced capital and intermediate goods. See Mahalanobis (1955a, 1955b).

10. See Sen and Ray (2015).

11. Normally, we would expect the employment elasticity to be lower in modern (large-scale) manufacturing than in traditional (small-scale) manufacturing, but the reverse was the case during 2000–12.

12. See Ghose (2016), chapter 7.

13. In Korea, for example, manufacturing was far more employment-intensive than services in 1963; manufacturing accounted for 4 per cent of GDP but 8 per cent of employment in the economy, while services accounted for 70 per cent of GDP but 26 per cent of employment. During 1963–90 (the period of Korea's transformation through rapid manufacturing-led growth), however, the employment elasticity was 0.53 in manufacturing and 0.84 in services. The same pattern is observed in the economic history of China, Japan, Taiwan, and other early industrializers of Europe.

14. See Ghose (2015) for evidence.

5

Future of Employment

The Outlook and the Challenge

India has thus far achieved far more growth than development. Very substantial economic growth over a period of seventy odd years has brought only very slow improvement in employment conditions. Worse, growth accelerations did not bring speedier improvement in employment conditions. Fundamentally, the pattern of growth has throughout been biased against use of labour, particularly of low-skilled labour—India's most abundant resource.

Employment conditions in India, consequently, still remain poor.[1] In the first place, only 52 per cent of the adult population is in the labour force, a fact that itself indicates scarcity of job opportunities for the low–skilled.[2] The average quality of employment is also poor. Just over 7 per cent of the employed workers is in formal employment or 'good jobs'. The modern sector, defined broadly to include all public and private corporate sector establishments and the private non-corporate sector establishments employing at least ten workers, employs less than 18 per cent of the workers. And about 60 per cent of those employed in the modern sector are non-formal employees. A large section of the workers, 33 per cent, is in casual wage employment. A much larger section, 47 per cent, is in self-employment, mostly with a poor asset base. Underemployment is high; only 37 per cent of the casual labourers and 67 per cent of the self-employed have full-time work. More than 12 per cent of all employed workers are effectively in surplus in the sense that they can be moved out of their current employment without producing any adverse effect on output.

The employment challenge that India now faces is clearly formidable (Tables 5.1 and 5.2). There is a backlog of 79 million persons—60 million currently employed but surplus workers and 19 million currently unemployed—who will need to be provided with productive jobs.[3] On the conservative assumption that the labour force participation rate will remain unchanged at the current level (52.2 per cent), around 7 million persons will be joining the labour force

Table 5.1 Projected population and labour force (numbers in million)

	2018	2035 (a)	2035 (b)
Adult (15+) population			
Male	506.1	623.6	623.6
Female	477.0	592.2	592.2
Total	983.1	1215.8	1215.8
Adult (15+) labour force			
Male	382.2	471.0	471.0
Female	130.6	162.1	177.7
Total	512.8	633.1	648.7
Annual addition to labour force			
Male		5.2	5.2
Female		1.9	2.8
Total		7.1	8.0
Labour Force Participation Rate (%)			
Male	75.5	75.5	75.5
Female	27.4	27.4	30.0
Total	52.2	52.1	53.4

Source: Author's estimates based on labour force statistics from Labour Bureau survey and data on projected adult population available from the UN Population Division.

Notes: (a) Estimate based on the assumption that the female labour force participation rate will remain unchanged at the level observed in 2016; (b) Estimate based on the assumption that the female labour force participation rate will rise to 30 per cent in 2035.

Table 5.2 India's employment challenge (numbers in million)

	2018	2018–35 (a)	2018–35 (b)
Employed but surplus workers	60		
Unemployed	19		
The backlog	79		
New entrants into labour force		120	136
Job creation required		199	215
Job creation required, per annum		12	13

Source: Author's estimates based on labour force statistics from Labour Bureau survey and data on projected adult population available from the UN Population Division.

Notes: The underlying assumptions are (a) that employment conditions in 2018 were no different from those in 2016, and (b) that there will be no surplus workers or unemployed persons in 2035.

annually between 2018 and 2035. A more reasonable assumption, however, is that women's participation rate will gradually increase from 27.5 per cent, the current level, to 30 per cent in 2035, while men's participation rate will remain unchanged at the current level (75.5 per cent). Women's participation rate is now abysmally low. Also, there are grounds for believing that an important reason why many women have been staying out of the labour force is non-availability of jobs of acceptable quality. It is reasonable to expect that many will move into the labour force as jobs of acceptable quality become available. Faster creation of productive jobs, in other words, will itself increase women's labour force participation. On the assumption of rising labour force participation of women, the overall participation rate will gradually rise to 53.4 per cent in 2035, labour force growth will be 1.4 per cent per annum, and the number joining the labour force annually between 2018 and 2035 will be about 8 million.

To see the enormity of the jobs challenge, we can consider a modest goal of reaching what is known as the Lewis Turning point—the point at which there are no surplus workers or unemployed—by 2035. This would require absorption of 215 million persons—79 million currently surplus and unemployed workers and 136 million who will be joining the labour force—in productive jobs between now and 2035. This means that around 12.5 million jobs will need to be created in each of the years between now and 2035. These jobs, it needs to be emphasized, have to be productive so that decent incomes can be earned from them. This indeed is where the challenge is. In India, jobs create themselves to a significant extent. But these are very low-productivity jobs. Creation of such jobs does not pose much of a challenge but also does nothing to improve employment conditions in the country.

The employment challenge, it must also be said, is not just one of creating 12.5 million productive jobs per year but also one of ensuring that many of these jobs are for low-skilled workers. India's labour force is overwhelmingly low-skilled and will remain so for quite a long time to come. In 2016, according to the Labour Bureau Survey, just about 34 per cent of India's labour force had completed secondary or higher-level education. Based on past trends, less than 50 per cent will have done so by 2035. India will need to create productive jobs for millions of low-skilled workers, many of whom are already present in the labour force and many more who will be joining the labour force between now and 2035. It cannot 'leapfrog' into becoming a high-skill economy by 2035. Or, rather, it can do so only by keeping a very large section of its workers engaged in low-productivity work and/or unemployed or even out of the labour force, thereby keeping a large section of its population mired in poverty.

All this does not mean that there is no need to create jobs for skilled workers. The proportion of persons with secondary or higher-level education in India's labour force will be rising and job opportunities for them will need to expand. Otherwise, open unemployment of the 'young and educated' will steadily rise. The challenge is not one of job creation exclusively for the low-skilled or exclusively for the high-skilled. India will have to 'walk on two legs'. But the need to create jobs for the low-skilled deserves to be emphasized because it has remained largely unrecognized; the past pattern of growth has not just been inadequately job-creating but has also been strongly biased in favour of job creation for skilled workers. Innovation is required to alter the pattern so that growth becomes much more job-creating and also creates jobs for both low-skilled and skilled workers.

Meeting the Challenge

Can the jobs challenge be met? If so, how? These are central issues of economic policy in today's India.

An important point to note in this context is that not all the jobs that need to be created have to be entirely new. Substantial improvement in the productivity of many of the currently existing jobs in the traditional sector, particularly in agriculture, can also count as creation of productive jobs and there is much scope for doing this. Improving labour productivity in agriculture will require on the one hand achieving decent growth of agricultural output and on the other ensuring negative or at least zero growth of the workforce in the sector by facilitating outmigration of workers into productive jobs in non-agriculture, preferably into modern non-agriculture. Non-agriculture, modern non-agriculture in particular, is where new productive jobs will need to be created. We can see the rough orders of magnitude. At a minimum, the number of new jobs to be created in non-agriculture annually will have to be large enough to absorb the fresh entrants into the labour force and a fraction of the backlog (the currently employed but surplus workers and the currently unemployed). This then will mean zero growth of the workforce in agriculture and declining share of agriculture in total employment. Agricultural growth of 3 per cent per annum, if achieved and sustained, can then translate into productivity growth of 3 per cent per annum. This, by reducing underemployment and increasing labour incomes, will effectively move some of the workers currently underemployed or employed in very low-productivity activities to higher-productivity jobs within agriculture every year.

To ensure zero growth of the workforce in agriculture, around 11 million new productive jobs (for 8 million new labour force entrants and 3 million from the stock of unemployed and surplus workers) will need to be created annually in non-agriculture over the seventeen years between 2018 and 2035. This looks like a tall order in light of India's own recent experience. Between 2000 and 2012, when *non-agriculture excluding construction* grew at an annual rate of 8.4 per cent, just 4.6 million new jobs were created annually in the sector. Another 2.7 million new jobs were created annually in construction, but a significant proportion of these jobs was created through public works programmes and a large-scale special employment scheme—the Mahatma Gandhi National Rural Employment Guarantee Scheme (MGNREGS)—that began its career in 2005. So, while non-agricultural jobs increased by more than 7 million annually, not all of these jobs were created by non-agricultural growth. Moreover, not all of these additional jobs were productive; a significant proportion of the new non-agricultural jobs was of poor quality, involving engagement in low-productivity activities either as self-employed or as casual workers.

To see if and how the challenge of creating 11 million productive jobs in non-agriculture annually can be met, it is useful to reframe the problem. India's non-agricultural workforce in 2016 stood at 254 million—55 million in construction and 199 million in the rest of non-agriculture. If employment in agriculture is to record zero growth during 2016–35 and if there is to be zero unemployment and zero surplus labour by 2035, non-agricultural employment must increase to 425 million by 2035. On the assumption that the rate of growth of employment in construction during 2016–35 will be the same as that achieved during 2012–16 (2.1 per cent per annum), construction will employ around 82 million workers in 2035.[4] Employment in *non-agriculture excluding construction* will then have to be about 343 million in 2035. Thus, employment in *non-agriculture excluding construction* will need to grow at 2.9 per cent per annum between 2016 and 2035. If the employment elasticity for this period is the same as that observed for the period 2000–12 (that is, 0.321), the required growth of *non-agriculture excluding construction* would be 9 per cent per annum, which is higher than what was achieved during 2000–12 (8.4 per cent per annum). If, on the other hand, *non-agriculture excluding construction* grows at 8.4 per cent per annum during 2016–35, then the employment elasticity will need to be 0.345, which is larger than that observed during 2000–12.

These numbers deliver a crucially important message: even if the pace and pattern of non-agricultural growth of the period 2000–12 can be reproduced for the period 2018–35, the employment challenge will not be met. If the challenge is to be met, either the pace of growth of *non-agriculture excluding construction* will have to be significantly faster than 8.4 per cent per annum, or the employment elasticity of non-agricultural growth will have to be substantially larger than 0.321, or both growth and employment elasticity will have to be higher. The question is: How can these objectives be achieved? The short answer is that a transition from services-led growth to manufacturing-led growth will be required. The reasons are: rapid services-led non-agricultural growth is most unlikely to be attainable in future; the employment elasticity of this kind of growth is most likely to decline; and job creation will remain seriously biased against low-skilled workers. On the other hand, there are good reasons to think that rapid manufacturing-led growth is possible, that the employment elasticity of this kind of growth will be higher, and that this kind of growth will create jobs for both low-skilled and high-skilled workers.

It needs to be recognized that rapid non-agricultural growth (at even 8 per cent per annum) will in fact be hard to sustain if growth remains services-led. As argued earlier, services-led growth has not really been driven by export-oriented dynamic services; it has been consumption-led growth driven by inflows of foreign finance, which have been generating high income growth for the already rich. Sustainability of this growth has been and remains contingent on continuation of large inflows of foreign finance. The fundamental reason for this dependence is the growing imbalance between domestic absorption (consumption plus investment) requiring mainly goods and domestic production supplying mainly services. Large and growing trade deficit is thus an inherent feature of this growth process, and the dependence on foreign capital derives from the need to finance the trade deficit. Thus, foreign finance has been critical to growth from both the demand side and the supply side. It is hard to see how growth of this kind can be sustained for very long. Growing income inequality will begin to have adverse effect on the growth of aggregate demand in the economy causing slowdown of economic growth. And inflow of foreign capital that will be required to finance the large and growing trade deficit cannot be taken for granted. Non-agricultural growth, if it continues to be services-led, is most likely to be significantly slower in future.

The past experience suggests, moreover, that the employment elasticity of this kind of growth, already low, will decline further essentially because skill-intensive services will continue to grow faster than employment-intensive services. This also means that the bias in job creation against low-skilled workers will very probably grow stronger. So, even if services-led growth of non-agriculture could, by some miracle, be sustained at 9 per cent per annum, this would still not help in meeting the employment challenge.

There are several good reasons to think, on the other hand, that a transition to manufacturing-led growth will bring the desired growth acceleration. In the first place, growth of manufacturing is what is required to reduce the imbalance between domestic absorption (consumption plus investment) and domestic production, and thus to reduce the persistently high trade deficit and the consequent dependence on foreign finance. The proper role of foreign capital is to finance investment and not consumption and trade deficit. And foreign capital can play its proper role only when it is not required to finance persistently high trade deficit. As the imbalance between domestic absorption and domestic production is progressively reduced and trade deficit grows smaller, foreign capital can increasingly finance investment (rather than trade deficit), thereby raising the investment rate in the economy and helping growth acceleration. Moreover, when foreign capital finances investment, it will create jobs and contribute to growth of aggregate demand rather than to growth of income inequality.

Second, manufacturing remains really undeveloped in India. Indeed, strange though it may seem, India is one of the least industrialized countries not just in Asia but in the world. Since the early 1980s, the share of manufacturing in India's GDP has hovered at 16 per cent without showing any rising trend. The share of manufacturing in total employment in the economy has hovered at 12 per cent without showing any rising trend. This state of underdevelopment of manufacturing, however, also holds a promise: the scope for expansion remains large and rapid growth of manufacturing seems eminently possible.

Third, the traditional strengths of manufacturing remain relevant (see Box 4.1 in Chapter 4). Increasing returns to scale in production, high tradability of products, high income elasticity of demand at low levels of income and ability to employ low-skilled labour at a productivity premium are still there. Growth of manufacturing can thus be faster than growth of any other sector. Growth of manufacturing also has strong spillover effects on other sectors of the economy generating growth stimulus for those sectors. While certain services have also acquired some (though not all) of these characteristics of manufacturing, they account for too small a share of the national output to be as powerful a growth engine as manufacturing. At any rate, such dynamic and export-oriented services can continue to grow even when growth is manufacturing-led.

Apart from bringing growth acceleration, a transition from services-led growth to manufacturing-led growth will also increase the employment elasticity of non-agricultural growth and will thus be helpful in meeting the employment challenge. In the first place, the employment elasticity ought to be and in fact has been larger in manufacturing than in services. Of particular importance is the fact that in recent periods, the employment elasticity has been larger in modern manufacturing than in modern services. If future growth of manufacturing is geared to production for both domestic and export markets, the employment elasticity can be expected to increase further.

Moreover, in India, the share of low-skilled workers in total workforce is much higher in modern manufacturing than in modern services.[5] A transition from services-led growth to manufacturing-led growth will thus help generate speedier growth of productive jobs for low-skilled workers in non-agriculture generally and in the modern sector in particular.

Fourth, services growth itself can be expected to become more employment-intensive when non-agricultural growth is manufacturing-led than when it is services-led. India's own past experience as also the experience of other successful developers strongly suggests such an outcome. The reason is that growth of manufacturing stimulates growth of relatively employment-intensive services such as trade and transport. Under a services-led growth regime, the relatively skill-intensive services grow faster so that the employment elasticity tends to decline.

Finally, physical infrastructure is of much greater relevance for manufacturing-led growth than for services-led growth. A transition from services-led growth to manufacturing-led growth, therefore, will call for faster development of physical infrastructure. This will mean faster growth of construction, a highly low-skilled labour-intensive industry.

Manufacturing-Led Growth in the Twenty-First Century

It is often argued today that the potential benefits of manufacturing-led growth at early stages of development are unlikely to be available in the twenty-first century, when the so-called Fourth Industrial Revolution is on course and the patterns of trade are likely to be changing.

The technologies associated with the Fourth Industrial Revolution (robotics, 3D printing, internet of things, artificial intelligence, and machine learning), it is argued, are rapidly eroding the traditional strengths of manufacturing, namely, the relatively high labour intensity and the ability to employ low-skilled labour at a productivity premium. These technologies also have the potential of changing the pattern of international trade by altering the basis for comparative advantage. If technology transforms the traditionally labour-intensive manufactures into skill-intensive manufactures, for example, the comparative advantage of low-income countries arising from abundant supply of low-skilled labour and low wage may simply disappear. Some assessment of these possibilities needs to be made in order to see if there is still a case for manufacturing-led growth. Two caveats are in order. First, any such assessment cannot but be somewhat tentative because full development and widespread adoption of the new technologies are yet to happen. Second, the new technologies will have consequences not just for manufacturing but also for services so that the appropriate assessment is a comparative one, which, however, is difficult to conduct at this stage.

The threat to low-skill jobs in labour-intensive manufacturing arises from the possibility of automation created by technologies such as robotics and 3D printing. From what we know, however, automation has been a significant trend in only a few manufacturing sub-sectors and these sub-sectors happen to be capital- and skill-intensive.[6] A large number of sub-sectors that are labour-intensive and actually account for the bulk of manufacturing employment in developing countries have not witnessed much automation.[7] The traditional strength of manufacturing—the ability to employ low-skilled labour at a productivity premium—survives more or less unscathed and, the evidence indicates, will survive in the foreseeable future.[8] We cannot say, of course, that this will remain so for ever. But this is

142

not an argument against the pursuit of manufacturing-led development today. There is nothing to be gained by not availing of the developmental benefits of manufacturing over the next fifteen to twenty years even if it is the case that these benefits will no longer be there in some distant future.

How might the new technologies affect the trading patterns? There are two mutually contradictory possibilities. The technologies associated with the Third Industrial Revolution (basically computers, the internet, and mobile phones) hugely expanded trade by promoting fragmentation of manufacturing thereby increasing the scope for trade in intermediates (parts and components). Some of the technologies associated with the Fourth Industrial Revolution represent advances on the earlier technologies and could further increase the scope for trade in intermediates thereby expanding the global value chains. On the other hand, automation may restore the developed countries' comparative advantage in certain products thereby promoting reshoring. However, given that automation is prominent basically in capital- and skill-intensive manufactures, not all of which are highly traded, the scope for such reshoring is most likely to be quite limited.

The best judgement that can be made at this point of time is that the developmental benefits of manufacturing will remain available for at least a few decades to come. This means that India still has the opportunity to pursue manufacturing-led growth and thereby transform not just its economy but also its employment conditions. Rapid manufacturing-led growth will bring rapid development. The opportunity must not be missed.

Notes

1. The ratios and proportions cited here are derived from data generated by the Labour Bureau Survey and thus are those observed for 2016 rather than for 2018.
2. Compare this with the labour force participation rate in China, which was 71 per cent in 2016.
3. The term 'job' is often used to refer to paid employment. Throughout this chapter, we use the term to refer to all types of productive work.
4. Employment generated through MGNREGS stopped growing after 2012. Growth of employment in construction declined from 8.8 per cent during 2000–12 to 2.1 per cent during 2012–16. If we assume that employment generated through MGNREGS or any other special employment scheme is unlikely to expand beyond the level achieved in 2012, we can reasonably suppose employment in construction to grow at 2.1 per cent in future.
5. See Ghose (2016) for evidence.

6. Examples are transport equipment, consumer electronics, electrical machinery, and equipment.
7. These include highly traded labour-intensive manufacturing such as textiles, garments, and leather goods, and less traded commodity-based manufacturing such as food and beverages.
8. These conclusions emerge from a careful and comprehensive analysis of the issues and evidence in Hallward-Driemeier and Nayyar (2018). Very similar findings relating to India's manufacturing industry are reported in Mani (2019).

Epilogue

The availability of new data on employment from a recent NSSO survey[1] now allows us to make a fuller assessment of the changes in employment conditions that occurred after 2012. What emerges is that the trends observed for the period 2000–12 persisted, some even strengthened, during 2012–18. Labour force growth continued to decelerate as the labour force participation rate continued to decline. Employment growth also continued to decelerate and actually turned negative (it had already turned negative during 2012–16). What might look like a new trend is a sharp rise in the rate of unemployment, but this too can be seen to have resulted from developments that had already been under way in the earlier period and continued into the later period (indeed, the rate of unemployment had already increased during 2012–16). Alongside these trends, as happened during 2000–12, the average quality of employment in the economy improved. In both periods, moreover, this improvement was, to a significant extent, a consequence of the withdrawal of the 'poor and low-skilled' from the labour force, which was associated with progressive disappearance of non-formal jobs. But the scale of withdrawal of the low-skilled and the associated disappearance of non-formal jobs was far larger during 2012–18 than during 2000–12. India's employment problem has been worsening, but this now shows up more in trends in labour force participation and unemployment than in trends in incidence of poor-quality jobs and underemployment.

Labour Force, Employment, and Unemployment

One striking fact is that labour force growth decelerated very sharply—from 1.3 per cent per annum during 2000–12 to just 0.2 per cent per annum during 2012–18—even while the growth of the adult population decelerated only a little—from 2.1 per cent per annum during 2000–12 to 1.8 per cent per annum during 2012–18 (Table E.1). The reason, of course, is a sharp decline in the labour force participation rate, from 56 per cent in 2012 to 50 per cent in 2018 (Table E.2). We may recall that the labour force participation rate had

Table E.1 Population, labour force, and employment

	Numbers in million			Growth (%)	
	2000	2012	2018	2000–12	2012–18
Population (15+)	687.3	883.6	983.1	2.1	1.8
Labour force (15+)	420.3	490.3	495.0	1.3	0.2
Employment (15+)	410.1	479.9	465.3	1.3	−0.5

Source: Author's estimates.

Note: The data on population (15+) are taken from the UN Population Division database. The estimates of labour force and employment are derived by multiplying the ratios of labour force to population and employment to population, available from NSSO surveys.

Table E.2 Labour force participation rates by level of education

	Male		Female		Person	
	2012	2018	2012	2018	2012	2018
Not literate	87.6	79.8	38.4	27.8	55.7	46.3
Up to primary	89.2	86.5	32.4	25.2	62.9	56.7
Middle	78.4	77.9	24.1	17.8	55.5	52.1
Secondary and above	70.9	68.7	21.7	20.3	51.5	49.3
All persons	79.2	75.7	30.3	23.4	55.5	50.4

Source: Author's estimates based on data available from the NSSO surveys.

declined fairly sharply between 2000 and 2012 as well (from 61 per cent to 56 per cent) and that this decline is explained only in small part by the increased pursuit of education and in large part by the withdrawal of women with little or no education from the labour force. The decline in labour force participation between 2012 and 2018 resulted in large part from withdrawal of both men and women with little or no education from the labour force. If job opportunities were shrinking for low-skilled women during 2000–12, they were shrinking for the low-skilled in general during 2012–18.

A second important fact is that the deceleration in employment growth—from 1.3 per cent per annum between 2000 and 2012 to -0.5 per cent per annum between 2012 and 2018—was much sharper than the deceleration in labour force growth. This is significant in that it points to a new development: a decoupling of employment growth from labour force growth. Between 1955 and 2012, as we have seen, employment growth almost always equalled labour force growth basically because the scope for work sharing had remained wide. During 2012–18, however, the scope for work sharing (in casual labour and self-employment) seems to have been shrinking so that the employment growth was significantly lower than the labour force growth.

So, the unemployment rate, which had remained low and stable till 2012, recorded a fairly sharp increase—from just 2 per cent in 2012 to 6 per cent in 2018. As always, unemployment was high for the educated and insignificant for persons with little or no education even in 2018 (Table E.3). But even for persons with middle-level education, unemployment has now become significant. The unemployment rate for the educated (that is, of persons with secondary or higher education) was also much higher in 2018 than in 2012. These facts indicate two developments. The first is that the growth of formal jobs failed to keep pace with the growth in the number of the educated

Table E.3 Unemployment and labour force by level of education

	Unemployment rate (%)		Per cent of labour force	
	2012	2018	2012	2018
Not literate	0.4	1.2	29.9	24.6
Up to primary	1.1	2.7	23.1	18.8
Middle	2.1	5.5	16.5	21.1
Secondary and above	4.9	11.3	30.5	35.5
All persons	2.1	6.0	100.0	100.0

Source: Author's estimates based on data available from the NSSO surveys.

looking for such jobs. As a matter of fact, between 2012 and 2018, the number of persons with secondary or higher education in the labour force increased by 19 million while the number of formal jobs increased by 15 million (Tables E.3 and E.4). Moreover, not all of the incremental formal jobs were new; some were newly formalized non-formal jobs that already existed. Second, the higher unemployment of both the educated and those with middle-level education also indicates growing scarcity of jobs even in the traditional sector. As a matter of fact, non-formal employment actually recorded a significant decline (see Table E.4). This means a significant decline in employment in the traditional sector.

However, increased unemployment of the educated was not the only factor behind the sharp increase in the overall unemployment rate. The other reason was the rapid increase in the share of the educated in the labour force. The share of persons with secondary or higher education in the labour force increased from 31 per cent in 2012 to 36 per cent in 2018. The share of persons with middle-level education also increased from 17 per cent in 2012 to 21 per cent in 2018. These increases were due not just to the rising average level of education of the adult population but also because of the much sharper decline in the labour force participation of the less educated than in that of the

Table E.4 Structure of employment

	Per cent of employed		Growth (%)
	2012	2018	2012–18
Type of employment			
Formal employment	8.0	11.5	5.6
Regular employment	9.9	11.3	1.7
Casual employment	29.8	24.9	−3.5
Self-employment	52.3	52.3	−0.6
Non-formal employment	92.0	88.5	−1.2
Sector of employment			
Agriculture	48.8	44.1	−2.2
Manufacturing	12.6	12.1	−1.2
Construction	10.6	11.7	1.1
Mining and utilities	1.0	1.0	−0.6
Services	27.0	31.1	1.8

Source: Author's estimates based on data available from the NSSO surveys.

Note: Data relate to total employment (which includes a small number of child workers) and not to employment of adults (15+). The estimates for 2012 are now comparable to those for 2018 but are slightly different from those for 2012 discussed in Chapter 3, which related to employment of adults.

educated. Indeed, we observe a neat inverse relation between the magnitude of decline in labour force participation and the level of education. Between 2012 and 2018, for example, the labour force participation rate declined by 9 percentage points for persons with no education but by only 2 percentage points for persons with secondary or higher education.

The most important point that emerges from the scrutiny is that manifestations of the employment problem have been changing. Till 2000, inadequate growth of employment opportunities showed up basically in growth of low-productivity jobs and of underemployment. After 2000, inadequate growth of employment opportunities began to manifest itself more in declining labour force participation of the low-skilled than in growth of low-productivity jobs and of underemployment. After 2012, declining labour force participation became the principal manifestation of inadequate growth of employment opportunities for the low-skilled while increasing open unemployment became the principal manifestation of inadequate growth of employment opportunities for the educated. Changes in employment conditions can now be read from observed trends in participation and unemployment rates.

Employment Conditions

While labour force participation declined and unemployment increased, the average quality of employment in the economy improved during 2012–18. We may recall that during 2000–12 too labour force participation had declined and the average quality of jobs had improved. In both periods, casual wage employment declined while formal employment increased but the magnitudes were larger in the second period. Between 2012 and 2018, the share of casual employment in total employment declined from 30 per cent to 25 per cent, the share of formal employment increased from 8 per cent to 12 per cent and the share of regular employment increased from 10 to 11 per cent, while the share of self-employment remained unchanged (Table E.3). The employment quality index, which had increased from 1.893 in 2000 to 1.972 in 2012, increased further to 2.094 in 2018.

Unlike during 2000–12, however, the increase in formal employment during 2012–18 was accompanied by a decline in non-formal employment. In the earlier period, formal employment had increased by 8 million and non-formal employment had increased by 62 million so that total employment had increased by 70 million. Between 2012 and 2018, however, formal employment increased by 15 million while non-formal employment declined by 31 million so that total employment in the economy declined by 16 million. These facts suggest that in the later period many of the incremental formal jobs were newly formalized non-formal jobs and not new formal jobs. They also suggest that while some of the non-formal jobs were transformed into formal jobs, many non-formal jobs were simply lost. The loss of many non-formal jobs, it might be noted, went together with the withdrawal of many of the low-skilled from the labour force. So, during 2012–18, the average quality of jobs in the economy improved not so much because there was large movement of workers from low-productivity to high-productivity jobs as because there was large movement of low-skilled workers from low-productivity jobs to no jobs (indeed to the category of out of the labour force).

A very similar picture emerges from a scrutiny of employment growth by sector (Table E.4). Between 2012 and 2018, employment in agriculture declined by about 30 million while that in non-agriculture increased by just 14 million. Clearly, many low-skilled agricultural workers moved from agricultural jobs to no jobs rather than to non-agricultural jobs.

In fact, employment of the low-skilled increased only in construction during 2012–18. Employment in the sector increased by over 3 million and, as we know, casual wage employment is the overwhelmingly dominant form of employment in the sector. In *non-agriculture excluding construction*, employment increased by nearly 11 million (employment actually declined by 4 million in manufacturing and increased by 15 million in services). Since formal employment, which increased by 15 million, can be expected to have increased basically in non-agriculture excluding construction (this is what is observed to have happened during 2000–12), non-formal employment in the sector must have declined by 4 million. So, the average quality of employment in the sector improved not just because of growth of better-quality jobs but also due to the destruction of poorer-quality jobs.

The same happened in agriculture. While many jobs disappeared, the average quality of employment in the sector improved quite significantly during 2012–18. For one thing, the declining importance of casual wage employment implies declining underemployment. For another, output per worker in agriculture grew at 5 per cent per annum and this should have led to a healthy growth of real labour incomes of the self-employed and the casual workers. Indeed, the evidence suggests that the real daily wage of casual labour in rural India increased at a rate of 4 per cent per annum during 2012–18.[2]

Did employment conditions improve or deteriorate during 2012–18? The answer clearly is: they deteriorated. Many non-formal jobs disappeared leading to large-scale exit of the low-skilled from the labour force. Expansion of opportunities for formal employment was woefully inadequate causing a sharp rise in unemployment of the educated. While the average job quality improved, the improvement is attributable basically to large-scale loss of low-productivity jobs and not to significant movement of workers from low-productivity to high-productivity jobs.

The Challenge

The employment challenge that confronts India now appears even more formidable than that outlined in Chapter 5 (see Table E.5). The backlog changes only in composition; the stock of surplus workers is lower (50 million) while the stock of unemployed is higher (29 million). On the conservative assumption that the labour force participation rates of both men and women will remain unchanged at the current levels, about 7 million persons will be joining the labour force annually between 2018 and 2035. On the more reasonable assumption that women's participation rate will gradually increase from 23.4 per cent, the current level, to 30 per cent in 2035 while men's participation rate will remain unchanged at the current level (75.7 per cent), the number joining the labour force annually will be 9 million and the labour force will be growing at 1.6 per cent per annum.

Table E.5 India's employment challenge (numbers in million)

	2018	2018–35 (a)	2018–35 (b)
Employed but surplus workers	50		
Unemployed	29		
Backlog	79		
New entrants into labour force		116	155
Job creation required		195	234
Job creation required, per annum		12	14

Source: Author's estimates based on data from (*a*) UN Population Division database for projected population and (*b*) from NSSO survey for the rest.

Therefore, if the Lewis Turning Point is to be reached by 2035, around 13 million (between 12 and 14 million) productive jobs, many of them for the low-skilled, will need to be created annually. If the workforce in agriculture is to remain the same as in 2018 and if unemployment and surplus labour are to fall to zero by 2035, employment in non-agriculture will need to increase from 265 million in 2018 to 486 million in 2035. If it is assumed that employment growth in construction during 2018–35 will be the same as that during 2012–18, construction will employ

67 million in 2035. So, employment in non-agriculture excluding construction will have to increase from 209 million in 2018 to 419 million in 2035. This means that employment in non-agriculture excluding construction will need to grow at 4.2 per cent per annum. If we suppose that the employment elasticity will be what it was observed to be during 2000–12 (that is, 0.321), the required growth rate of output is nearly 13 per cent per annum. On the other hand, if the output growth is 8.4 per cent per annum (that is, what it was during 2012–18), the required value of employment elasticity is 0.5. The clear message is: if the pace and pattern of growth of non-agriculture excluding construction observed during 2000–12 were to be reproduced during 2018–35, the employment challenge will not be met. The pace of growth will have to be faster and the pattern of growth will need to change so that the employment elasticity is significantly larger.

Notes

1. 'Annual Report: Periodic Labour Force Survey, July 2017–June 2018' (National Statistical Office, Ministry of Statistics and Programme Implementation, Government of India).
2. This finding, based on data from the NSSO surveys, appears to be somewhat at odds with the finding

reported in Himanshu (2017) but in broad accord with that reported in Kundu (2018), both of which use data from a different source (Labour Bureau).

References

Chancel, L., and T. Piketty. 2017. 'Indian Income Inequality, 1922–2014: From British Raj to Billionaire Raj?'. WID (World Inequality Database) Working Paper Series no. 2017/11.

Dasgupta, S., and A. Singh. 2007. 'Manufacturing, Services and Premature Deindustrialisation in Developing Countries: A Kaldorian Analysis'. In *Advancing Development: Core Themes in Global Economics*, edited by G. Mavrotas and A. Shorrocks. London: Palgrave Macmillan.

Datt, Gaurav. 1998. 'Poverty in India and Indian States: An Update'. FCND Discussion Paper no. 47. International Food Policy Research Institute, Washington, D.C.

Ghose, A.K. 2015. 'Services-Led Growth and Employment in India'. In *Labour, Employment and Economic Growth in India*, edited by K.V. Ramaswamy. New Delhi: Cambridge University Press.

———. 2016. *India Employment Report 2016: Challenges and the Imperatives of Manufacturing-Led Growth*. New Delhi: Oxford University Press.

Hallward-Driemeier, Mary, and Gaurav Nayyar. 2018. *Trouble in the Making? The Future of Manufacturing-Led Development*. Washington D.C.: World Bank.

Himanshu. 2017. 'Growth, Structural Change and Wages in India: Recent Trends'. *The Indian Journal of Labour Economics* 60(3): 309–31.

Kaldor, N. 1967. *Strategic Factors in Economic Development*. Ithaca: Cornell University Press.

Kochar, K., U. Kumar, R. Rajan, A. Subramanian, and T. Tokatlidis. 2006. 'India's Pattern of Development: What Happened, What Follows?'. *Journal of Monetary Economics*, 53(5): 981–1019.

Kotwal, A., B. Ramaswami, and W. Wadhwa. 2011. 'Economic Liberalization and Indian Economic Growth: What's the Evidence?'. *Journal of Economic Literature* 49(4): 1152–99.

Kundu, S. 2018. 'Rural Wage Dynamics in India: What Role Does Inflation Play?'. RBI WPS (DEPR): 03/2018.

Lewis, W.A. 1954. 'Economic Development with Unlimited Supplies of Labour'. *The Manchester School* 22(2): 139–91

Mahalanobis, P.C. 1955a. 'The Approach of Operational Research to Planning in India'. *Sankhya* 10: 3–62. Reproduced in *P.C. Mahalanobis: Papers on Planning*, edited by P.K. Bose and M. Mukherjee. Calcutta: Statistical Publishing Society, 1985.

———. 1955b. 'Approach to Planning in India'. Radio Talk. Reproduced in *P.C. Mahalanobis: Papers on Planning*, edited by P.K. Bose and M. Mukherjee. Calcutta: Statistical Publishing Society, 1985.

———. 1958. 'Science and National Planning'. *Sankhya* 20: 69–106. Reproduced in *P.C. Mahalanobis: Papers on Planning* edited by P.K. Bose and M. Mukherjee. Calcutta: Statistical Publishing Society.

Mani, S. 2019. 'Robot Apocalypse: How Will Automation Affect India's Manufacturing Industry'. *Economic and Political Weekly* 54(8): 40–8.

Rodrik, D., and A. Subramanian. 2005. 'From "Hindu Growth" to Productivity Surge: The Mystery of the Indian Growth Transition'. *IMF Staff Papers* 52(2): 193–228.

Sen, Abhijit. 1991. 'Shocks and Instabilities in an Agriculture-Constrained Economy, India 1964–1985'. In *Rural Transformation in Asia*, edited by J. Breman and S. Mundle. New Delhi: Oxford University Press.

Sen, Anindya, and P. Ray. 2015. 'The Ascent and Decline of Reservation in Indian Small Scale Industries: Evolution of the Policy Environment'. WPS no. 759, Indian Institute of Management Calcutta.

Further Readings

Basu, K. 1984. 'The Enigma of India's Arrival: A Review of Arvind Virmani's *Propelling India: From Socialist Stagnation to Global Power*'. *Journal of Economic Literature* 46(2): 396–406.

Balakrishnan, P. 2010. *Economic Growth in India: History and Prospect*. New Delhi: Oxford University Press.

Chakravarty, S. 1987. *Development Planning: The Indian Experience*. Oxford: Clarendon Press.

Joshi, V. 2016. *India's Long Road: The Search for Prosperity*. Penguin Allen Lane.

Joshi, V., and I.M.D. Little. 1994. *India: Macroeconomics and Political Economy, 1964–1991*. Washington, D.C.: World Bank.

———. 1996. *India's Economic Reforms, 1991–2001*. Oxford: Oxford University Press.

Mohan, Rakesh. 2002. 'Small-Scale Industry Policy in India: A Critical Evaluation'. In *Economic Policy Reforms and the Indian Economy*, edited by A.O. Krueger. Chicago: University of Chicago Press.

Nayyar, D. 2006. 'India's Unfinished Journey: Transforming Growth into Development'. *Modern Asian Studies* 40(3): 797–832.

Panagariya, A. 2004. 'Growth and Reforms during 1980s and 1990s'. *Economic and Political Weekly* 39(2): 2581–94.

———. 2008. *India: The Emerging Giant*. Oxford and New York: Oxford University Press.

Index

About the Author

Ajit K. Ghose received his PhD in economics from the University of Cambridge, UK. He was a research fellow at Queen Elizabeth House, University of Oxford, UK, before joining the International Labour Organisation (ILO), Geneva, Switzerland, as a research economist in 1979. He retired from the post of a senior economist at the ILO in 2008. During 2009–10, he was Visiting Senior Fellow at Wolfson College, Cambridge, and at the Centre for Development Studies, University of Cambridge. During 2015–2017, he was a National Fellow of the Indian Council of Social Science Research. Currently, he is Visiting Professor, Institute for Human Development, New Delhi.

He has authored several books and many articles in professional journals, in areas such as agrarian transformation, globalization, inequality, economic growth and development, employment and labour markets, and poverty and famines. His latest major publication is *India Employment Report 2016: Challenges and the Imperative of Manufacturing-Led Growth* (Oxford University Press, 2016).